Edited by Naomi Starkey

Suggestions for using New Daylight

Set aside a regular time and place, if possible, when you can read and pray undisturbed. Before you begin, take time to be still and, if you find it helpful, use the BRF prayer. Read the Bible passage slowly—if the passage is over familiar, try reading it aloud for a change—and then turn to the comment.

The prayer, question or point for reflection can be a basis for your own meditation and prayers. You may find it helpful to keep a journal to record your thoughts about the passage or comment, or to note items for prayer.

Another way of using New Daylight is to meet with others to discuss the material, either regularly or occasionally. If you are using it as group material, you could simply share your responses to the Bible passaage, comment, prayer or point for reflection—or all three! Alternatively, you could use the subject matter as a starting point for your group's own wider study.

In New Daylight the Sundays and special festivals from the Church calendar are noted on the relevant days. This offers a chance to recall or get acquainted with the rich traditions of the Christian year.

Naomi Starkey

Writers in this issue

Peter Graves is Minister of Wesley Methodist Church, Cambridge, and Chaplain to Methodist students at the University. He was formerly Superintendent of the Methodist Central Hall, Westminster. He is the author of BRF's *Living and Praying the Lord's Prayer*.

Rob Gillion is Vicar of Upper Chelsea, London, and Evangelism Adviser for the Bishop of Kensington. He broadcasts regularly both nationally and locally, including BBC Radio's *Pause for Thought*. He was formerly a parish priest and prison chaplain in Hong Kong, also responsible for religious broadcasting.

Adrian Plass is an internationally popular writer and speaker in many countries. His most recent book for BRF is *When You Walk*.

David Spriggs is a Baptist minister, currently working as Head of Church Relations for Bible Society, where he has also been Project Director for The Open Book. He has written *Feasting on God's Word* for BRF.

David Winter is retired from parish ministry. An honorary Canon of Christ Church, Oxford, he is well known as a writer and broadcaster. He is the author of BRF's Advent book for 2003, *Hope in the Wilderness*. He is a Series Editor of *The People's Bible Commentary*.

Veronica Zundel is an Oxford graduate, writer and journalist. She lives with her husband and young son in North London, where they belong to the Mennonite Church.

Jenny Robertson lived for a number of years in Russia, working alongside her husband in St Petersburg. She has written many books for both adults and children, including *Strength of the Hills* for BRF. She has also had a number of books of poetry published.

Margaret Cundiff has worked in the Church of England since 1973, as a lay worker, deaconess, deacon and finally priest. She also broadcasts regularly and serves as Diocesan Mothers' Union Chaplain in the York Diocese. Her most recent book for BRF is *Still Time for Eternity*.

Christine Chapman was Director of Counselling for the Chester diocese. She is currently a member of the North-West Inter-Diocesan Counselling Team for clergy and their families, and is a lay Reader in her church.

Naomi Starkey writes...

Week by week, in church, many of us hear, 'This is the word of the Lord—thanks be to God.' When we turn to some parts of the Bible, however, we can wonder whether those words are appropriate. While we may find comfort, inspiration or reassurance in a reading from one of the Gospels or epistles, some parts of the Old Testament sound unpleasant, even stomach-turning or downright obscene!

Bible translators often go for the discreet options when translating parts of the text that are particularly graphic. In the Song of Songs, for example, the beloved praises the strength of her lover's 'body'—but I will leave you to find a commentary that spells out what she is actually admiring.

In other places, we can't avoid or draw a veil over the unpleasant facts. In one of Rob Gillion's readings from Genesis, he considers the story that has become legendary in the phrase 'the sin of Onan'. He shows how the biblical narrator is in fact making a wider point about disobedience rather than focusing on a specific sexual act.

Another very difficult part of the Bible is the book of Joshua. Veronica Zundel looks at chapters 7 to 12 of this troubling book, with its story that sounds uncannily similar to present-day newspaper headlines, echoing themes of ethnic cleansing, conflict and even genocide. There is no way of getting round the fact that in the process of settling in their promised land, the Israelites dispossessed many of the tribes already living there, apparently by divine command. While Veronica finds that this book can speak to us today, she shows how there are no easy answers, no readings that are not in some way unsettling.

If we believe that the Bible is a crucial part of God's revelation to us (the person of Jesus being, of course, the supreme revelation), we need to follow the example of Jacob. Genesis 32 tells how he wrestled all night long, eventually crying out to the stranger grappling with him, 'I will not let you go unless you bless me.' In the same way we need to wrestle with the difficult bits of the Bible, refusing to give up before we too receive a blessing—an insight into the God who inspired the original writers and guided those who later agreed the canon of scripture.

(P.S. By popular demand, we have reinstated the naming of each Sunday in the Church calendar.)

The BRF Prayer

Almighty God,
you have taught us that your word is a lamp for our feet
and a light for our path. Help us, and all who prayerfully
read your word, to deepen our fellowship with each other
through your love. And in so doing may we come to know you
more fully, love you more truly, and follow more faithfully in
the steps of your son Jesus Christ, who lives and reigns with
you and the Holy Spirit, one God for evermore. Amen.

1, 2 and 3 John

The first, second and third letters of John come from the same author. 1 John is a treatise or sermon written in the form of a general letter to the Church, while 2 and 3 John seek to apply the same message to specific situations. John the Presbyter (or Elder), who was a leader in the Church of Asia Minor wrote them. Scholars differ as to his exact identity. He could have been John the 'beloved disciple', but whoever he was, his approach is certainly very similar to that of John's Gospel.

Written towards the end of the first century, the letters address a different community setting than that of the Fourth Gospel. Whereas the Gospel addresses those who have been excluded from the synagogue because of their belief in the pre-existent and divine Son of God, the epistles are not concerned with Jewish traditions. Rather, they emphasize the physical reality of Jesus and oppose the teaching of former members of the Church who, having been influenced by Gnostic teaching, have broken away.

To the Gnostics, only the spiritual world was real. As the material world was evil and imaginary it needed to be conquered by the spiritual. They claimed perfection, believing that they had superior knowledge (*gnosis*) to that of the Church. Proudly self-conscious, they engaged in schismatic preaching in the churches. Many of the New Testament epistles directly oppose Gnostic teaching as it denied the essential truths of the gospel, including the significance of the coming of Jesus in the flesh, and the saving power of the cross.

Some Gnostics—the Docetists (or 'seemists')—believed that as matter was, by definition, evil, Jesus could not possibly have had a body, he only seemed to! Moral decisions between good and bad were blurred and did not matter as they only seemed to be important. The doctrine of Christian love was also scoffed at. People didn't really need sympathy, care and affection, they only seemed to.

John's epistles, therefore, stress the reality of the humanity of Jesus, the difference between good and evil and the victory over worldly attitudes and values that can be ours if we have faith in Christ, who alone is the source of all faith and true knowledge. They are powerful letters that challenge us to walk in the light of truth and love. They have much to say to our contemporary situation.

Peter Graves

7

Fully human

We declare to you what was from the beginning, what we have heard, what we have seen with our eyes, what we have looked at and touched with our hands, concerning the word of life—this life was revealed, and we have seen it and testify to it, and declare to you the eternal life that was with the Father and was revealed to us—we declare to you what we have seen and heard so that you also may have fellowship with us; and truly our fellowship is with the Father and with his Son Jesus Christ.

Christianity stands or falls on who Jesus is. A Jesus who was not fully human would have been irrelevant to the human condition. If he were not also truly divine, he would have been inadequate to bring us salvation from sin and death. Christian theology, therefore, has always seen Jesus as both God and human.

This epistle is written against the background of a Gnostic heresy that regarded only the spiritual as real and the material world as imaginary and evil. If Jesus really were the spiritual Son of God, he could not possibly have had a real human body as, by definition, a body, being material, must be evil. Jesus could only have 'seemed' to have had a body. Such heretics came to be known as 'Docetists' or 'Seemists'. 1 John tackles this belief head on. 'The Word' really 'became flesh and lived among us' (John 1:14), so much so that he could be heard, seen and touched.

Unlike the greeting of other New Testament letters, this epistle begins with a prologue clearly linked to that in John's Gospel. Indeed, he is writing a kind of brief commentary on the Gospel prologue with special emphasis on the fullness of Christ's humanity.

Unlike our watered-down understanding of 'fellowship', the New Testament concept is very rich. It involves partnership, communion and mutual indwelling! As we 'abide' in Christ, we have fellowship with the Father and our fellow Christians. The aim of discipleship is that we have an in-depth relationship with God and each other. This emphasis also reflects the teaching of John's Gospel (see John 15:7–10 and 17:21–23).

Prayer

Thank you, Lord, for being both God and human so that we can enjoy a new living and ever-growing relationship with you.

PG

1 JOHN 1:5–7 (NRSV)

Walk in the light

This is the message we have heard from him and proclaim to you, that God is light and in him there is no darkness at all. If we say that we have fellowship with him while we are walking in darkness, we lie and do not do what is true; but if we walk in the light as he himself is in the light, we have fellowship with one another, and the blood of Jesus his Son cleanses us from all sin.

Writing of his experiences in a Lebanese prison, Terry Waite speaks of the comfort and reassurance that came to him from a shaft of light that penetrated the darkness of his cell. Cruel humans might do their worst. His captors might break his body, but his soul was not theirs to possess. Nothing could extinguish the light of truth that comes from God himself.

Although surrounded by the darkness of ignorance, fear and sin, we know that light has been revealed in Christ, enabling us to catch a glimpse into the very heart of God. Jesus also shows us how to live the life abundant and so fulfil our human potential by becoming more and more like him.

Light is one of the most powerful of all religious symbols. It not only points to the goal of our existence, but also shows us the path to follow so that we can attain it. Having seen the light, we can discern the folly of darkness more clearly. It illumines the dangers and pitfalls that forever seek to entice and trap us. Thus we know what must be avoided if we are to be the people God intends.

Our calling is to authentic discipleship. Right belief must lead to right action. We cannot live a lie. To continue walking in darkness leads to alienation from God and our fellow human beings. Lacking any sense of direction, we find ourselves lost in a confusing world. On the other hand, to walk in the light leads to an ever-deepening relationship with God, our fellows and our innermost selves. Darkness is thwarted and the light of Christ transforms us.

Meditation

Refining fire, go through my heart,
Illuminate my soul;
Scatter thy life in every part,
And sanctify the whole.

Charles Wesley (1707–88)
PG

1 John 1:8—2:2 (NRSV, abridged)

Facing failure and finding forgiveness

If we say that we have no sin, we deceive ourselves, and the truth is not in us. If we confess our sins, he who is faithful and just will forgive us our sins and cleanse us from all unrighteousness. If we say that we have not sinned, we make him a liar, and his word is not in us... if anyone does sin, we have an advocate with the Father, Jesus Christ the righteous; and he is the atoning sacrifice for our sins.

To claim to walk in the light when our deeds are evil is to live a lie. As light and darkness are opposites, coming to the light involves the exposure of all that we are to the searchlight of his transforming love. The denial of our sinfulness prevents us from receiving help. We lie to ourselves and, by denying his assessment of our situation, we also make God himself a liar. It is only when we face the seriousness of sin, confess it and acknowledge our need, that we are ready to receive the salvation and healing God offers.

In this epistle, John is wrestling with a serious dilemma. He is sure that, through the cross, sin has been conquered and, therefore, those who have claimed his victory and received salvation should not sin. Why then is it so obvious that even in committed Christians, sin is still very much alive? John recognizes that, having been conquered, sin needs to be rooted out as we journey towards holiness.

Such growth in discipleship naturally takes time. Accordingly, he emphasizes the need for ongoing confession and forgiveness. The more we grow, the more we see our need for further cleansing and renewal.

Jesus is the 'advocate' who has stood by our side and assured us of salvation. He is also the 'atoning sacrifice' who cleanses us and heals our broken relationship with God. Thus, when we do sin and find ourselves taking a step backwards, we need to confess it and seek forgiveness. Then, by his grace and in the strength of his spirit, we determine to take two steps forward as we continue our journey towards holiness.

Prayer

Help me, Lord, to acknowledge my need of you. Show me how to grow through my failures and learn from them. Teach me to move forward in faith.

PG

1 JOHN 2:15–17 (NRSV)

Eternal questions

Do not love the world or the things in the world. The love of the Father is not in those who love the world; for all that is in the world—the desire of the flesh, the desire of the eyes, the pride in riches—comes not from the Father but from the world. And the world and its desire are passing away, but those who do the will of God live forever.

Sometimes this passage has been used to reinforce the cultural baggage of a particular denomination or tradition by stressing the 'worldly' things we must refrain from or condemn. It is sad that some Christians define themselves by what they don't do rather than by the faith that motivates them. It is not refusing to drink, gamble or swear that makes us Christians. Surely discipleship is seen in our commitment to Christ, a living faith, and the desire to further the work of his kingdom.

One of the great things about Sunday worship is that it helps us to reflect on the focus of our lives and what is really important to us. John has just praised his readers for all they have experienced in their pilgrimage of faith (vv. 12–14). To love God, know the forgiveness of sins, experience victory over evil and find strength by abiding in his word is of course good. Nevertheless, such blessings do not excuse us from answering the important questions that confront us. What are we living for? In what

do we put our trust? Do we really want the things of God or do we lust after the things of this world such as sex, money and power? Although given high status in our culture, such worldly things can be dangerous. They can divert us from the eternal truths of the gospel into backwaters that lead nowhere.

When Christ is the centre of our lives, everything else fits into place and lesser things eventually fade into insignificance. No wonder Jesus challenges us to 'strive first for the kingdom of God and his righteousness' (Matthew 6:33). That's the secret of victory!

Sunday reflection

Riches I heed not,
nor man's empty praise;
Be thou mine inheritance
now and always;
Be thou and thou only
the first in my heart:
O Sovereign of heaven,
my treasure thou art.

Irish, c. 8th century, trans. Mary Byrne

PG

Children of God

See what love the Father has given us, that we should be called children of God; and that is what we are. The reason the world does not know us is that it did not know him. Beloved, we are God's children now; what we will be has not yet been revealed. What we do know is this: when he is revealed, we will be like him, for we will see him as he is.

In the 19th century, Billy Bray, the great and powerful Cornish evangelist, was often criticized for his lack of breeding and formal education. None of this was important to him. He was 'the son of a King' and that was the only thing that mattered. It gave him all the status he needed. Just as the world did not recognize Jesus as the Son of God, so we should not be surprised that we are not recognized as his children. Nevertheless we are still children of the King, a fact that nothing can destroy.

Made by the creator God, we are all his creatures, but by grace alone we can become the children of God. As we respond to his generous love and gracious invitation, we enter a living relationship with the Father. The richness and security of this relationship removes all fear of the unknown future. It is enough to know that he holds it in his hands and so all will be well.

Although we cannot know what heaven is really like until we get there, John does give us some clues. He tells us that when Jesus is revealed in glory, we shall be like him. Made in the image of God, our true humanity was distorted by the fall. By his example Jesus shows us how we were meant to live. When in eternity we meet him face to face, we will see as never before how we were meant to live. In heaven we will catch a vision of God, so that, seeing him as he is, we can become more like him and that surely is the goal of Christian spirituality.

Meditation

More of thy glory let me see,
Thou holy wise and true!
I would thy living image be,
In joy and sorrow too.

Johan Caspar Lavater (1741–1801)

PG

The test of discipleship

Little children, let us love, not in word or speech, but in truth and action... And this is his commandment, that we should believe in the name of his Son Jesus Christ and love one another, just as he has commanded us. All who obey his commandments abide in him, and he abides in them. And by this we know that he abides in us, by the Spirit that he has given us.

To be the children of God involves living rightly and putting love into practice. Sometimes, though, we wonder how Christian we really are. Aware of our own weak faith, mixed motives and inadequate discipleship, there are bound to be times when our conscience condemns us. Those who feel burdened by a sense of guilt or failure will find a word of reassurance in our passage here. As God is bigger than our feelings, he not only sees our sins but also our highest aspirations and ideals. He understands our deepest emotions, our loves, longings and dreams and wants to help rather than condemn (see vv. 19–22).

The test of our discipleship, therefore, is not our feelings. They usually tell us far more about our inner life and current situation than they do about God. Instead John emphasizes the need to believe, love and obey, for in so doing we abide in Christ.

Hebrew names reflect the nature and character of a person. To believe in the 'name' of Jesus means that we accept him for who he really is. From such belief comes our motivation for love and obedience. Love both for God and our fellows is the guiding principle of Christian discipleship, and the subject of our Lord's great commandment—to love one another as he has loved us (John 15:12). Such belief and love leads naturally to obedience as, in gratitude, we long to please the God who has given us so much.

Obedience leads to mutual abiding as our relationship with Christ is deepened and enriched. Furthermore, the Holy Spirit reassures us of the indwelling presence of Christ no matter what we feel.

Prayer

Thank you, Lord, for your compassion and understanding. Enable me to rise above my feelings so that, through belief, love and obedience, I will abide in you and you in me.

PG

God is love

Beloved, let us love one another, because love is from God; everyone who loves is born of God and knows God. Whoever does not love does not know God, for God is love. God's love was revealed among us in this way: God sent his only Son into the world so that we might live through him. In this is love, not that we loved God but that he loved us and sent his Son to be the atoning sacrifice for our sins. Beloved, since God loved us so much, we also ought to love one another.

Love has always been central to Christian faith and life. Writing in the first century, Ignatius of Antioch said, 'The Christian life begins and ends with two qualities: faith which is the beginning, and love which is the goal.'

Our experience of God's love enables us to escape from our self-concern and live on a bigger map. Knowing God we learn to love, and by loving others we learn to know God. Made in the image of God, we are called to reflect his love in acts of selfless service. The more we do so, the more we discover the depths of the very nature of God himself, for he is love. Such love provides a motive for existence, a guide for action and a reason for courage. It draws the best from us and enables us to live life to the full. It is the essence of discipleship and the goal and purpose of our living.

An American surgeon had given up a lucrative practice at home to serve a mission hospital in East Asia. A visiting colleague watched him perform an exhausting seven-hour operation with inadequate equipment. Later, the visitor asked, 'At home that operation would have cost thousands. How much is it worth here?' The surgeon thought of his first meeting with the old woman when she was wheeled in, clutching a few small coins and begging his help. Then he replied, 'For this I will get her gratitude and my Master's smile, but that is worth more than all the praise and money that the world can give!'

Prayer

Teach me, Lord, the way of perfect love that I may 'know you more clearly, love you more dearly and follow you more nearly, now and forever'.

After Richard of Chichester (1197–1253)

PG

14

No fear in love

God is love, and those who abide in love abide in God, and God abides in them. Love has been perfected among us in this: that we may have boldness on the day of judgment, because as he is, so are we in this world. There is no fear in love, but perfect love casts out fear; for fear has to do with punishment, and whoever fears has not reached perfection in love. We love because he first loved us.

One of the fascinating things about the TV programme *Big Brother* is the glimpse we catch of both the private and public faces of the residents. When all together, some come across with confidence and bravado, but in private conversations with Big Brother or a particular friend they reveal their vulnerability and fears.

We all have our fears and many of them revolve around other people's perceptions of us. Will they like me? Will I be misunderstood? Will they find out about my weaknesses? Will they see through me and know what my motivations really are? Although such fears are natural, John reminds us that 'perfect love casts out fear'! Jesus can set us free from the prison of our own self-concern and so put our fears into perspective as he enables us to live life to the full.

With our friends we may seek to keep up appearances and that can be exhausting, but with God we can be transparently real. He knows us as we really are, so there is no point in pretending. Instead, we need to confess our sin honestly and acknowledge our need. Then we receive the salvation freely offered by the cross and so discover a deep sense of security. Even judgment need not be feared as Jesus has already born our punishment and given us the assurance of salvation.

God accepts us as we are, but loves us too much to leave us there. He forgives the past and enables us to move forward in trust and obedience. In gratitude for such a wonderful salvation, we offer our lives in loving service to others and face the future in hope and confidence.

Prayer

Thank you, Lord, for accepting me with all my fears and failings. Thank you for your perfect love that sets me free to be. Help me to express my gratitude in a life of self-giving love.

PG

2 John 5b–9 (NRSV, abridged)

Truth and love

Let us love one another. And this is love, that we walk according to his commandments; this is the commandment just as you have heard it from the beginning—you must walk in it. Many deceivers have gone out into the world, those who do not confess that Jesus Christ has come in the flesh… Be on your guard… Everyone who does not abide in the teaching of Christ, but goes beyond it, does not have God; whoever abides in the teaching has both the Father and the Son.

This letter is written by the same author as 1 John and deals with the same problem. There are some who would lead the Church away from sound doctrine into what they regarded as more progressive, sophisticated and advanced. Although Christian doctrine should not be considered static, it must be centred on a correct understanding of the reality of Christ. The Son of God did actually become human and this must be the touchstone of all our thinking. Indeed, that which is not in tune with Jesus can never be right. We do not follow some vague nebulous, undefined philosophy, but rather serve a God who revealed himself in the flesh and blood Jesus of Nazareth.

When John Wesley was asked to define his doctrine of Christian holiness or sanctification, he said that if we were looking for anything other than 'perfect love' we were looking wide of the mark. It is not the seeking of some special experience or new knowledge that leads us to perfection. Rather, it is love for God and our fellows that is all-important. Such love involves our need to constantly abide in Jesus so that he can abide in us. From this relationship of mutual indwelling, true growth takes place and we move forward on the road to holiness.

Although love must be at the heart of all our actions, this does not mean that we have to be wishy-washy and neglect sound doctrine. We are also called to follow the truth. God has revealed himself in Christ and we cannot improve on such truth, no matter how modern or progressive our ideas might sound. It is not the latest bright idea, but the truth that sets us free!

Prayer

Lord, help me to follow your truth, and live the life of love.

PG

Walk in the truth

I was overjoyed when some of the friends arrived and testified to your faithfulness to the truth, namely how you walk in the truth. I have no greater joy than this, to hear that my children are walking in the truth... Beloved, do not imitate what is evil but imitate what is good. Whoever does good is from God; whoever does evil has not seen God.

This third letter of John is written to Gaius, a respected and influential member of the Church. It pleads for hospitality for visiting Christian missionaries as this is part of our calling to love one another. One of the Church leaders, Diotrephes, needs to be challenged. He is so convinced of his own importance that he not only refuses to offer hospitality himself, but even prevents and excludes those who do want to be welcoming. He is sharply contrasted with Demetrius who does walk in truth. Whereas the second letter urges readers not to give hospitality to heretics as their presence disturbs the Church, now the situation has changed. The important difference is the truth of the doctrine that is preached and the loving example of the preacher. It must be authentically Christian and recognize the authority and centrality of Christ.

Here we see the joy of the pastor when people have caught the vision and live it. They 'walk in the truth'. Such truth is not something just for intellectual assimilation. It is the knowledge that fills our minds and helps us think and act in a Christ-like way.

These letters recognize that the company we keep influences us. We are challenged to 'imitate' what is good. This does not mean that, in some artificial or external way, we should become pale copies of those we imitate. Rather, it involves a willingness to be inspired by and learn from the example of those who really are worthy role models because they do walk in the truth. From their life, teaching and example, we are encouraged and from them we catch new insights into the truth of the gospel.

Prayer

Thank you, Lord, for all those whose example has inspired me to walk in the truth. Help me so to abide in you that my example will help and inspire others.

PG

What's in a name?

Then they moved on from Bethel. While they were still some distance from Ephrath, Rachel began to give birth and had great difficulty. And as she was having great difficulty in childbirth, the midwife said to her, 'Don't be afraid, for you have another son.' As she breathed her last—for she was dying—she named her son Ben-Oni. But his father named him Benjamin. So Rachel died and was buried on the way to Ephrath (that is, Bethlehem). Over her tomb Jacob set up a pillar, and to this day that pillar marks Rachel's tomb.

When we were waiting for the birth of our first child we spent time looking through the books of baby names trying to decide on something, but when he was born we knew just what to call him. His name was also confirmed by the nurses. We named him Alexander. My wife had a very difficult labour that lasted many hours until at last he was delivered safely. He weighed in at 10lb 2oz and on his chart the nurses added 'the Great'!

Rachel, too, had a difficult time, so difficult that it was to end in her death. Understandably, she focused on her own trauma rather than on the child. Yet out of that death came new life, although no child would want to go through life knowing he was Ben-Oni ('son of my trouble'). Perhaps he would blame himself for his mother's death, believing that trouble was his name and therefore trouble would be his nature. Fortunately his father Jacob knew she had

named him out of her pain and distress and gave him a name to give him confidence: Benjamin ('son of my right hand'). Benjamin would grow up knowing how much confidence his dad put in him.

Jacob had grown up with a name that meant 'deceiver'. God was to give him a new name, Israel, meaning 'someone who perseveres'. God was equally careful in choosing his son's name, Jesus. He was to be a saviour by name and by nature!

One of the greatest gifts you can give any child is the knowledge that they are loved and very special.

Sunday reflection

And a voice came from heaven:
'You are my Son, whom I love;
with you I am well pleased.'
(Mark 1:11)

ROBG

Family ties

This is the account of Esau (that is, Edom). Esau took his wives from the women of Canaan: Adah daughter of Elon the Hittite, and Oholibamah daughter of Anah... also Basemath daughter of Ishmael and sister of Nebaioth. Adah bore Eliphaz to Esau, Basemath bore Reuel, and Oholibamah bore Jeush, Jalam and Korah. These were the sons of Esau, who were born to him in Canaan. Esau took his wives and sons and daughters and all the members of his household, as well as his livestock and all his other animals and all the goods he had acquired in Canaan, and moved to a land some distance from his brother Jacob. Their possessions were too great for them to remain together; the land where they were staying could not support them both because of their livestock. So Esau (that is, Edom) settled in the hill country of Seir.

It wasn't easy to be inspired by this chapter full of genealogies. Mind you, a few of my relatives do get surprisingly inspired researching our family tree. I'm proud of some of our ancestors, such as the king of the Isle of Mull, 'Ghilean the Battleaxe', whereas Thomas Gillion, the horse thief, I'd rather forget! But past generations and history do have an important function.

Genesis is concerned with tracing Israel's ancestral line and in Edom they saw their nearest relative, Israel's twin brother Esau. The question was why he was passed over by his younger brother, Jacob, 'the deceiver'. The ancestral line tells us that Esau married a Canaanite girl, which showed his disrespect for his people—he also left the Promised Land because he couldn't live alongside his brother, who was 'too blessed'. These are all choices either to be obedient to God and serve him or focus on one's own selfish desires. At the end of the previous chapter, however, there is a hint of reconciliation when they come together to bury Isaac their father (35:29). I believe that it is important to put generational difficulties out of court and seek for reconciliation—whether your brother or sister be a king or a horse thief.

Reflection
I looked and there before me was a great multitude that no one could count, from every nation, tribe, people and language, standing before the throne and in front of the Lamb.
(Revelation 7:9)

ROBG

Sibling rivalry

This is the account of Jacob. Joseph, a young man of 17, was tending the flocks with his brothers... Now Israel loved Joseph more than any of his other sons, because he had been born to him in his old age; and he made a richly ornamented robe for him. When his brothers saw that their father loved him more than any of them, they hated him and could not speak a kind word to him. Joseph had a dream, and when he told it to his brothers, they hated him all the more. He said to them, 'Listen to this dream I had: We were binding sheaves of corn out in the field when suddenly my sheaf rose and stood upright, while your sheaves... bowed down to it.' His brothers said to him, 'Do you intend to reign over us? Will you actually rule us?' And they hated him all the more because of his dream and what he had said.

Joseph's story begins bathed in hatred. Joseph's brothers 'hated' him because he told their father about their bad behaviour. They 'hated' him because he was their father's favourite. They 'hated' him for his dreams, which to them reflected his arrogance. Although the dreams were a gift from God, his brothers were blinded by jealousy, which eventually caused their downfall. It is interesting to note that this story is presented as the family history of Jacob. In other words the storyteller is interested in all the sons of Jacob, but even the narrative favours Joseph.

Here we see the dire effects of hatred on human behaviour. I have an elder brother, 18 months older than me. As teenagers we certainly had our differences! We were often competing for attention, but if I was ever in trouble he was the first to defend me and come to my support. Jacob's favouritism turns normal brotherly rivalry into deadly hatred. The tragic effect of this hatred blights the life of Jacob's family for more than 20 years. The family is torn apart by hatred and grief, and the rest of the story is an unfolding of God's purposes to resolve the enmity and to bring unity to the family.

Reflection

And we know that in all things God works for the good of those who love him, who have been called according to his purpose.
Romans 8:28)

ROBG

The pit

So Joseph went after his brothers and found them near Dothan. But they saw him in the distance, and before he reached them, they plotted to kill him. 'Here comes that dreamer!' they said to each other. 'Come now, let's kill him and throw him into one of these cisterns and say that a ferocious animal devoured him. Then we'll see what comes of his dreams.' When Reuben heard this, he tried to rescue him from their hands. 'Let's not take his life,' he said. 'Don't shed any blood. Throw him into this cistern here in the desert, but don't lay a hand on him.' Reuben said this to rescue him from them and take him back to his father. So when Joseph came to his brothers, they stripped him of his robe—the richly ornamented robe he was wearing—and they took him and threw him into the cistern. Now the cistern was empty; there was no water in it.

Here, salt is rubbed into the brothers' wounds when Joseph arrives with provisions and wearing the 'richly ornamented' coat—a reminder of the special affection his father has for him (v. 3). Indeed, so deep was their hatred that they could not 'speak peaceably' (v. 4, AV) to him. There has always been a childhood saying that I could never cope with: 'sticks and stones may break your bones, but words will never hurt you'. That simply is not true.

The remark that they could not 'speak peaceably' foreshadows the whole story of Joseph and the loss of peace between members of the family. As we read yesterday, they hated him 'all the more' (v. 8). This is one of several plays on Joseph's name, which means 'added to'. Jacob is obviously unaware of the animosity and lack of peace in his own family. Only the intervention of Reuben, his eldest brother, saves Joseph from being murdered. When your friends and family turn against you it is particularly painful. Joseph is stripped and dumped for dead in a pit. His brothers then callously sit down to eat the lunch he had brought them from their father.

Reflection

*They struck [Jesus] on the head...
and spat on him.... they took off
the purple robe... Then they led
him out to crucify him.*
(Mark 15:19–20)

ROBG

Rescued

Judah said to his brothers, '...Come, let's sell him to the Ishmaelites...' His brothers agreed. So... his brothers... sold him for 20 shekels of silver to the Ishmaelites, who took him to Egypt. When Reuben returned... and saw that Joseph was not there, he tore his clothes. He went back to his brothers and said, 'The boy isn't there! Where can I turn now?' Then they got Joseph's robe, slaughtered a goat and dipped the robe in the blood. They took the ornamented robe back to their father... He recognized it and said, 'It is my son's robe! Some ferocious animal has devoured him. Joseph has surely been torn to pieces.' ... So his father wept for him.

The story continues to be seen through the eyes of Joseph's brothers, the eyes of jealousy, which, as we all know, is a very destructive emotion, more so when experienced collectively. Those who teach in schools know how easy it is for peer pressure to be exerted and students to exhibit behaviour that does not match their individual personality. What disturbs us most is how a group or crowd can be encouraged to do something that as individuals they would not dream of doing. Those individuals who have the gift of leadership do well to think about how they use their charisma.

Here we see the contrast between the two older brothers—Reuben, who had persuaded his brothers to drop Joseph into a pit rather than to kill him, and Judah, who persuades the others to sell him. Reuben is compassionate, not so much for Joseph perhaps, but concerned at the distress it will cause his father, Jacob. All the others are well pleased when the slave-traders arrive and purchase Joseph, for now they can become rich, as well as getting rid of their brother!

This extraordinary rescue of Joseph suggests that God can work through anyone's family history! He can use all our experiences to bring his purposes to pass, experiences of both good and ill. God is indeed merciful but also is our judge and knows all the secrets of our hearts.

Reflection

As Joseph was betrayed by his brothers and sold for a few shekels, so too was Jesus betrayed and sold by his friend.

ROBG

GENESIS 38:1–10 (NIV, ABRIDGED)

Family disobedience

Judah... met the daughter of a Canaanite... He married her and lay with her; she... gave birth to a son, who was named Er. She conceived again and gave birth to a son and named him Onan. She gave birth to still another son and named him Shelah... Judah got a wife for Er, his firstborn, and her name was Tamar. But Er, Judah's firstborn, was wicked in the Lord's sight; so the Lord put him to death. Then Judah said to Onan, 'Lie with your brother's wife and fulfil your duty to her as a brother-in-law to produce offspring for your brother.' But Onan knew that the offspring would not be his; so whenever he lay with his brother's wife, he spilled his semen on the ground to keep from producing offspring for his brother. What he did was wicked in the Lord's sight; so he put him to death also.

Sometimes scripture can be so difficult. At first sight this piece of history seems to bear no relation to Joseph's story. It works on one level as a device to create suspense. In one of the plays of Agatha Christie, a hand in a black glove appears through the French windows but is never referred to again! Joseph has been sold into slavery and we are eager to know what happened to him, but I can detect an important thread running through this story—the danger of disobedience.

Joseph's obedience to God in the next chapter is in stark contrast to the disobedience of the generation described in this passage. Here we find them failing to obey God. Er errs and Onan refuses to provide descendants for his brother. The sin is disobedi-

ence, which results in death. Judah has witnessed two of his sons die as a result of disobedience to God, yet he continues to deceive others and misuse his authority. He becomes a changed man by the end of this story, however (44:18–34). We must remember that this is the story of the whole of Jacob's family and it shows that transformation can take place with even the most difficult of characters.

Reflection

'I tell you... unless you repent, you... will all perish.'
(Luke 13:5)

ROBG

Tamar's triumph

Judah then said to his daughter-in-law Tamar, 'Live as a widow in your father's house until my son Shelah grows up.' … [But Tamar] saw that, though Shelah had now grown up, she had not been given to him as his wife. When Judah saw her, he thought she was a prostitute… So… he slept with her… About three months later Judah was told, 'Your daughter-in-law Tamar is guilty of prostitution, and as a result she is now pregnant.' Judah said, 'Bring her out and have her burned to death!' … she sent a message to her father-in-law. 'I am pregnant by the man who owns these… See if you recognize whose seal and cord and staff these are.' Judah recognized them and said, 'She is more righteous than I, since I wouldn't give her to my son Shelah.' And he did not sleep with her again. When the time came for her to give birth, there were twin boys in her womb.

The general point of this episode is that justice will be done and that those who break their promises will be brought to book. Judah is not at that time a man of his word. With the death of his two sons he promises that Tamar may marry his youngest son Shelah when he comes of age. Judah does not honour that commitment, but Tamar is determined to continue Judah's family line.

At the end of this section of the story he confesses he was in error. In the same way, all the brothers will eventually admit their sin against Joseph. Despite failures and sins, repentance will result in a change of heart and a new start. So the story closes with a twin birth replacing, as it were, Judah's two lost sons, Er and Onan, with Zerah and Perez. From Perez's family Boaz was born who married Ruth (Ruth 4:11). Boaz was the ancestor of King David, who in turn was the forefather of 'Jesus, who is called Christ' (Matthew 1:6, 16). So this story, which at first sight seems so marginal to biblical history, records a vital link in saving history. Tamar, in her determination to have children, secured for Judah the honour of being part of the family line of both David and the Saviour of the world.

Reflection

'Repent, for the kingdom of heaven is near.'
(Matthew 4:17)

ROBG

The Lord is here

Now Joseph had been taken down to Egypt. Potiphar, an Egyptian who was one of Pharaoh's officials, the captain of the guard, bought him from the Ishmaelites... The Lord was with Joseph and he prospered, and he lived in the house of his Egyptian master. When his master saw that the Lord was with him and that the Lord gave him success in everything he did, Joseph found favour in his eyes and became his attendant. Potiphar put him in charge of his household, and he entrusted to his care everything he owned... the Lord blessed the household of the Egyptian because of Joseph. The blessing of the Lord was on everything Potiphar had, both in the house and in the field. So he left in Joseph's care everything he had; with Joseph in charge, he did not concern himself with anything except the food he ate.

At our service on a Sunday we often use a greeting to introduce the eucharistic prayer (when we break bread together). As the priest I say, 'The Lord is here', to which the people respond, 'His spirit is with us'. Here in Egypt, Joseph has been cast out from his family and sold into slavery. Things couldn't be much worse, but 'the Lord was with Joseph' (v. 2), so much so that his master Potiphar recognized it too and offered him more and more responsibility in his household.

The sign of someone who is in step with the Lord is that they are seen as trustworthy. The master entrusts a good steward to manage his affairs. In the same way, God entrusts his world to us and invites us to share in that responsibility.

Our treasure in the family of the Church is the gifts and talents of the people. Let us pray that we use these gifts wisely to the glory of God.

So much of the story of Joseph is focused on the use or misuse of power. In Joseph's younger days, his gift of dreams was used to lord it over his brothers, but by the end of the story, we discover a loving and forgiving man who simply wants to serve God's purposes.

Sunday reflection

'For where your treasure is, there your heart will be also.'
(Luke 12:34)

RobG

Temptation resisted

Now Joseph was well-built and handsome, and after a while his master's wife took notice of Joseph and said, 'Come to bed with me!' But he refused. 'With me in charge,' he told her, 'my master does not concern himself with anything in the house; everything he owns he has entrusted to my care. No one is greater in this house than I am. My master has withheld nothing from me except you, because you are his wife. How then could I do such a wicked thing and sin against God?' And though she spoke to Joseph day after day, he refused to go to bed with her or even to be with her.

Joseph has now got his feet firmly under the table. He is put in charge of almost every aspect of his master's life, except 'the food he ate' (v. 6)—if it were poisoned, Potiphar would lose his right-hand man. There is a wonderful group of people known as PAs (personal assistants), who manage busy executives' lives. Just occasionally, I sense that they may be taking on certain responsibilities that are not theirs. Recently I had one such person ring me up about her boss' marriage. She was arranging everything, including talking through the marriage service with me. At one stage in the conversation I wondered if she might stand in for her boss as I felt sure that the bride-to-be might be too busy to attend her own marriage service! I insisted on dealing with her boss directly.

Here we have Joseph taking on so many areas of responsibility for Potiphar that his wife 'takes notice' and invites Joseph to add a further responsibility. All her advances to him are rebuffed; he refuses to do 'such a wicked thing' (v. 9). Political and business expediency never justifies sinful action. Joseph recognizes that he must accept the responsibility to refrain from sin. To do so, as he discovers painfully, does not guarantee immediate success in earthly ventures and may even lead to greater hardships, but God gives Joseph the peace to endure it.

Reflection

'Peace I leave with you; my peace I give you. I do not give to you as the world gives. Do not let your hearts be troubled and do not be afraid.'
(John 14:27)

ROBG

Life's not fair

One day he [Joseph] went into the house to attend to his duties, and none of the household servants was inside. She [Potiphar's wife] caught him by his cloak and said, 'Come to bed with me!' But he left his cloak in her hand and ran out of the house... She kept his cloak beside her until his master came home. Then she told him this story: 'That Hebrew slave... came to me to make sport of me...' When his master heard the story... he burned with anger. Joseph's master took him and put him in prison, the place where the king's prisoners were confined. But while Joseph was there in the prison, the Lord was with him; he showed him kindness and granted him favour in the eyes of the prison warder. So the warder put Joseph in charge of all those held in the prison, and he was made responsible for all that was done there.

Despite being wrongfully accused of a very serious crime, Joseph is not executed. Perhaps Potiphar knew his wife better than she thought! He does, however, need to show loyalty to his wife, so casts his most valued servant into prison.

Life is not fair, but ultimately God is just and merciful. Once again we read that delightful phrase, 'the Lord was with him' (v. 21). Joseph does not show bitterness or anger for being imprisoned without cause. He remains steadfast and the qualities that made him shine in the eyes of Potiphar are still evident even in the trials and tribulations of prison life. So much so that the prison warden puts Joseph in charge of the other prisoners.

In a South American country there is a prison that is run on purely Christian discipline and values. The prisoners are given responsibility for their own behaviour and certain prisoners, who have shown leadership qualities, are given authority for the security of the prison—they lock each other up! It was one of the worst prisons in the country, but now it is a model of good practice. I'm sure those who had the vision for this work knew Joseph's story well.

Reflection

'I have told you these things, so that in me you may have peace. In this world you will have trouble. But take heart! I have overcome the world.'
(John 16:33)

RobG

Dreams

Some time later, the cupbearer and the baker of the king of Egypt offended their master... Pharaoh was angry with his two officials... and put them in custody... in the same prison where Joseph was confined. The captain of the guard assigned them to Joseph, and he attended them. After they had been in custody for some time, each of the two men—the cupbearer and the baker of the king of Egypt, who were being held in prison—had a dream the same night, and each dream had a meaning of its own. When Joseph came to them the next morning, he saw that they were dejected. So he asked Pharaoh's officials who were in custody with him in his master's house, 'Why are your faces so sad today?' 'We both had dreams,' they answered, 'but there is no one to interpret them.' Then Joseph said to them, 'Do not interpretations belong to God? Tell me your dreams.'

Once more we find Joseph treating everybody equally and he is now assigned to look after the imprisoned staff of the king of Egypt. He is always eager to serve others and use his gifts for the glory of God.

As chaplain to a high-security prison in Hong Kong for many years I have first-hand experience of incarceration and it is not generally a good place for rehabilitation or restoration, except when an exceptional prisoner is transformed by the love of Christ. One such prisoner I encountered, facing life imprisonment, was at first bitter and angry, but as a result of a chance meeting with a Christian prison visitor, who left him a Bible, and the encouragement of fellow Christian inmates, he experienced a miraculous change of heart. Not only did he change within, but he also changed others around him. He was baptized and is spending the rest of his sentence inspiring others, both prisoners and prison staff alike with his strong Christian faith. He has been in prison now for 34 years, but for the last six years, since his baptism, he tells me he has been free. His name is Joseph. Just like his namesake, his expression of concern leads his fellow prisoners to open their hearts to him.

Reflection

'So if the Son sets you free, you will be free indeed.'
(John 8:36)

ROBG

And more dreams

So the chief cupbearer told Joseph his dream... 'This is what it means,' Joseph said to him. '...Within three days Pharaoh will lift up your head and restore you to your position... But when all goes well with you, remember me and show me kindness; mention me to Pharaoh and get me out of this prison... When the chief baker saw that Joseph had given a favourable interpretation, he said to Joseph, 'I too had a dream...' 'This is what it means,' Joseph said. 'The three baskets are three days. Within three days Pharaoh will lift off your head and hang you on a tree....' Now the third day was Pharaoh's birthday, and he gave a feast for all his officials.... He restored the chief cupbearer to his position, so that he once again put the cup into Pharaoh's hand, but he hanged the chief baker, just as Joseph had said to them in his interpretation. The chief cupbearer, however, did not remember Joseph; he forgot him.

Joseph's first dreams got him into deep trouble. These dreams look as though they might lead to freedom. Joseph requests that he might be remembered to Pharaoh and pleads his innocence. In prison one of the greatest gifts is hope and Joseph's hope lies with God. It is most important to Joseph that the inspiration to interpret the dreams comes from God. Joseph's attitude is consistent with the rejection of the writers of the Old Testament of any occult practices. He simply relies on prophecy as a means of discovering God's will.

The number three dominates both dreams. The explanation is perfectly clear—in three days the cupbearer will be given his job back. Encouraged by this interpretation, the baker now shares his dream. Again Joseph can only tell the truth. The three baskets represent three days, but this time until death. This story once again affirms that the Lord is with Joseph and that this prison experience will be a stepping-stone to the palace, but his great hope and prayer to be released was left unanswered. Two lessons that Joseph is to learn are patience and to suffer for righteousness' sake. Once again Joseph's experience is an example for us all.

Reflection

'Father, if you are willing, take this cup from me; yet not my will, but yours be done.'
(Luke 22:42)

ROBG

GENESIS 41:25–33 (NIV, ABRIDGED)

Wake-up call

Then Joseph said to Pharaoh, '...God has revealed to Pharaoh what he is about to do. The seven good cows are seven years, and the seven good heads of grain are seven years... The seven lean, ugly cows that came up afterwards are seven years, and so are the seven worthless ears of corn scorched by the east wind: They are seven years of famine... Seven years of great abundance are coming throughout the land of Egypt, but seven years of famine will follow them. Then all the abundance in Egypt will be forgotten, and the famine will ravage the land... The reason the dream was given to Pharaoh in two forms is that the matter has been firmly decided by God, and God will do it soon. And now let Pharaoh look for a discerning and wise man and put him in charge of the land of Egypt.'

What I enjoy about this phase of Joseph's life is his confidence in the authority of God. He could so easily have embellished the interpretations of the dreams, but he interprets them with great clarity. Seven years of abundance and seven years of famine. The dreams have been given to Pharaoh twice, which implies a sense of urgency.

Joseph is quite magnificent for not only does he interpret the dream, but he also tells Pharaoh what and who he needs to overcome this impending disaster. The plan is good. Joseph has truly been transformed in character and stature, so he is now intelligent and wise and endowed, as Pharaoh is quick to acknowledge, with the spirit of God. You will have noticed that I have closed each day's reading with a reflection on the words of Jesus. Once more we see in Joseph what we see fully in Jesus. Just as all were commanded to make way for Joseph (v. 43), so 'at the name of Jesus every knee should bow' (Philippians 2:10). The hallmark of their leadership, however, is humility. We witness in Joseph an extraordinary sea change, from the precocious spoilt child whose arrogance so upset his brothers, to a man who recognizes that the key to true leadership is to be subject to God and obedient to him.

Reflection

Humble yourselves, therefore, under God's mighty hand, that he may lift you up in due time.
(1 Peter 5:6)

RobG

GENESIS 41:53–57 (NIV)

God's promise

The seven years of abundance in Egypt came to an end, and the seven years of famine began, just as Joseph had said. There was famine in all the other lands, but in the whole land of Egypt there was food. When all Egypt began to feel the famine, the people cried to Pharaoh for food. Then Pharaoh told all the Egyptians, 'Go to Joseph and do what he tells you.' When the famine had spread over the whole country, Joseph opened the storehouses and sold grain to the Egyptians, for the famine was severe throughout Egypt. And all the countries came to Egypt to buy grain from Joseph, because the famine was severe in all the world.

Pharaoh puts Joseph in charge of the whole land of Egypt. We have read how Joseph rises to the position of Potiphar's steward, then the prison governor's deputy and finally vizier of Egypt—next in authority to Pharaoh himself. He is put in charge of everything, including managing Egypt's food supplies. You may remember that, under Potiphar, Joseph was put in charge of everything except the food he ate. By contrast, the king of Egypt trusts him totally.

Once again, there are parallels with the life of Jesus. Young Joseph provides food for his brothers. Jesus breaks bread with his disciples. Joseph feeds the whole of Egypt, Jesus feeds the five thousand and brings the bread of life to the whole world. This story of Joseph began as the family history of Jacob and, in the same way, the life of Jesus is about God the Father, a God of love who wants the very best for us and promises to be with us always to the end of time. As we witness the disunity between Jacob's family members, we are reminded of how easy it is for the family of the Church to suffer in the same way. Jesus speaks with his Father: 'I pray… for those who will believe in me through their message, that all of them may be one' (John 17:20–21).

Prayer

Father, hallowed be your name, your kingdom come. Give us this day our daily bread. Forgive us our sins, for we also forgive everyone who sins against us. And lead us not into temptation. Amen.

ROBG

King Solomon

Solomon was the son of David and Bathsheba—clearly a man of talent and insight even before God specifically gifted him with yet greater wisdom. As he started to emerge as the most glorious of Israel's kings, David died, having passed on the plans for the temple to his son. Most of Solomon's reign (probably about 40 years) was a peaceful and prosperous period for Israel. Politically astute and very adept in his handling of people, the king amassed huge wealth and used much of it to construct the temple that his father had never been allowed to build. This magnificent construction was sited on Mount Moriah, the hill that had been Araunah's threshing floor, the place where God halted the plague that was about to devastate Jerusalem, as recorded in the first book of Chronicles. David offered a sacrifice here and bought the site for the temple. Mount Moriah was also the place where Abraham once prepared to sacrifice Isaac and, in the future, it was to be the hill to the north of the city where Jesus was crucified. Nowadays, the site is covered by the Dome of the Rock, one of Islam's holiest shrines.

In addition to building the temple, Solomon erected a palace for himself that took 13 years to build. There is reason to believe that this may have been even more sumptuous than the dwelling-place he designed and completed for God.

For many years, Solomon was a devoted follower of the one true God, continually praying and offering sacrifices on behalf of himself and his people. He was actually visited by God on at least two occasions and it would have seemed inconceivable in the early years that he could ever stray from the path of virtue. Perhaps because of the cumulative effects of such massive wealth and power, however, a time came when, as an old man, Solomon was seduced by his foreign wives into following gods such as Ashtoreth and Molech. Such foolishness is almost inexplicable in a man gifted with such wisdom, but it happened and it made God extremely angry. He punished Solomon by allowing only one tribe of Israel to be ruled by his son after Solomon's death.

What kind of man was Solomon? Well, as usual in the Bible, this kind of information lies both in the lines and between them, so that's where we'll look.

Adrian Plass

He was just and compassionate

At this, all Adonijah's guests rose in alarm and dispersed. But Adonijah, in fear of Solomon, went and took hold of the horns of the altar. Then Solomon was told, 'Adonijah is afraid of King Solomon and is clinging to the horns of the altar. He says, "Let King Solomon swear to me today that he will not put his servant to death with the sword."' Solomon replied, 'If he shows himself to be a worthy man, not a hair of his head will fall to the ground; but if evil is found in him, he will die.' Then King Solomon sent men, and they brought him down from the altar. And Adonijah came and bowed down to King Solomon, and Solomon said, 'Go to your home.'

Read from the beginning of this chapter to see how this little drama has unfolded. David's son Adonijah has set himself up as the one who will succeed David as king without any reference to David himself or to Nathan, the prophet who, years ago, had confronted David with his sin over Bathsheba and Uriah. Adonijah and his supporters are in the middle of a celebratory feast when they hear that Solomon has been made king. The feast breaks up in confusion. Adonijah is terrified, believing that his younger brother will certainly have him killed.

Why did Solomon not do exactly that? Adonijah, poorly disciplined by a father who was as weak with his sons as he had been strong in most other situations (see v. 6), was a genuine threat to the peace and stability of the new king's reign. Perhaps Solomon loved his brother.

Perhaps he didn't. Perhaps he wanted this first decision of his reign to be characterized by the best and finest qualities. Mercy and justice were the attributes of God himself. It was a time for new beginnings. If Adonijah behaved himself, there would be no reason for conflict or punishment in the future.

OK in theory, but, as we shall see presently in the case of Shimei son of Gera, theory and practice do not always coincide.

Prayer

Lord, let our actions reflect your heart when we deal with others. Let us be ready, whenever it is possible and right, to show compassion and forgiveness, even with those who may seek to do us harm.

AP

1 KINGS 2:8–9, 36–38 (NIV, ABRIDGED)

He kept his promises

'And remember, you have with you Shimei son of Gera... who called down bitter curses on me the day I went to Mahanaim. When he came down to meet me at the Jordan, I swore to him by the Lord: "I will not put you to death by the sword." But now, do not consider him innocent. You are a man of wisdom; you will know what to do to him. Bring his grey head down to the grave in blood.' ... Then the king sent for Shimei and said to him, 'Build yourself a house in Jerusalem and live there, but do not go anywhere else. The day you leave and cross the Kidron Valley, you can be sure you will die; your blood will be on your own head.'

One of Solomon's first tasks as king was to decide about his father's old enemies, like Joab and Shimei, both of whom had been allowed to live in David's lifetime. The first passage here details David's words to his son in the matter of Shimei. Perhaps his attitude was a compound of vengeful feelings and genuine fear for Solomon's welfare, but there was no doubt about the content of his advice. Shimei should be put to death.

Once more, why did Solomon not do this immediately? His kingdom could never be totally secure and at peace as long as these potentially subversive elements survived. However, intelligence and compassion tend to walk parallel paths. Perhaps he believed that it must be possible to arrive at an understanding with Shimei, although events had already driven him to command the execution of Adonijah,

his older brother, and Joab, who had once commanded the king's army.

Whatever the reason for this forbearance, he does his best for Shimei, just as we have seen him attempting a new beginning with Adonijah. He offers him a place to live and a promise that he will remain unharmed as long as he stays in Jerusalem.

The king certainly kept his promise. For three years Shimei stayed put, and not a hair of his head was harmed. He must have realized that the king's word could be trusted, but he made the mistake of forgetting the other, far more ominous promise that had been made.

Prayer

Lord, make us strong in our promises, accountable to you.

AP

He carried out his threats

When Solomon was told that Shimei had gone from Jerusalem to Gath and had returned, the king summoned Shimei and said to him, 'Did I not make you swear by the Lord and warn you, "On the day you leave to go anywhere else, you can be sure you will die"? At that time you said to me, "What you say is good. I will obey." Why then did you not keep your oath to the Lord and obey the command I gave you?' The king also said to Shemei, 'You know in your heart all the wrong you did to my father David. Now the Lord will repay you for your wrongdoing. But King Solomon will be blessed, and David's throne will remain secure before the Lord for ever.' Then the king gave the order to Benaiah son of Jehoiada, and he went out and struck Shimei down and killed him....

An intriguing story. I wish it were more detailed. What did Shimei say when he was tackled about his excursion to Gath? Did he try to justify himself? Did he claim that he'd forgotten the promise made three years ago?

'After all,' he might have argued, 'all I did was go and get a couple of runaway slaves back. Hardly a threat to your kingdom, is it?'

Of course, in itself, it wasn't. The fact was, though, that Shimei had disobeyed a direct order from the king and deliberately broken the terms of his suspended sentence. Did he think Solomon had not really meant what he said? Did he suspect that the king was soft, and would never actually carry out his threat? Had he convinced himself after three uneventful years in Jerusalem that a tiny infraction of the rule would barely be noticed? Was the man mad?

Infuriatingly, we shall have to wait until we meet Solomon before we know the answers to these questions. We know, though, that Solomon, faced with a potentially dangerous instability in the attitude and behaviour of this old enemy of his father's, now took the step David had advised in the first place. Shimei was executed.

The final threat to the stability of Solomon's kingdom had been removed.

Reflection

Is it easier to keep a promise to carry out a threat?

AP

He was wise (part 1)

That night God appeared to Solomon and said to him, 'Ask for whatever you want me to give you.' Solomon answered God, 'You have shown great kindness to David my father and have made me king in his place. Now, Lord God, let your promise to my father David be confirmed, for you have made me king over a people who are as numerous as the dust of the earth. Give me wisdom and knowledge, that I may lead this people, for who is able to govern this great people of yours?' God said to Solomon, 'Since this is your heart's desire and you have not asked for wealth, riches or honour, nor for the death of your enemies, and since you have not asked for a long life but for wisdom and knowledge to govern my people over whom I have made you king, therefore wisdom and knowledge will be given you.'

This is like a fairy story, isn't it? You know, the one where the hero gets three wishes and he makes disastrous mistakes with the first two before sorting it out at the third go.

Solomon made no mistakes. God gave him the wisdom he asked for, but this king's head must have been screwed on the right way before that, mustn't it? Instead of going for what most human beings want, he requested something that would enable him to perform adequately the huge task lying before him. As I mentioned last time I wrote about Solomon, he must have been sincere, because God would have known if he was only trying to impress. He got his wisdom and, if you read on, you'll see he was promised wealth, riches and honour as well. Jackpot! He'd won the lottery.

So, what would you choose? What would I choose? Well, actually, I know exactly what I'd choose, in fact have chosen already. It hasn't changed for years and I think I'm being given it in instalments. Peace—that's what I want most and, of course, there are many different things that come under that heading. There are things connected with faith and family and friends and the future. Total peace this side of heaven? I suspect not, but one day…

Do you dare to pray the prayer at the bottom of this page?

Prayer

Lord, the thing I want most in the world is…

AP

He was wise (part 2)

Then the king said, 'Bring me a sword.' So they brought a sword for the king. He then gave an order: 'Cut the living child in two and give half to one and half to the other.' The woman whose son was alive was filled with compassion for her son and said to the king, 'Please, my lord, give her the living baby! Don't kill him!' But the other said, 'Neither I nor you shall have him. Cut him in two!' Then the king gave his ruling: 'Give the living baby to the first woman. Do not kill him; she is his mother.'

Yes, Solomon was extremely wise, and here, in the story of two supplicant women and a baby, is the best-known illustration of that wisdom. A sparkling piece of decision making, but certain things occur to me.

First, it can only have been a one-off solution, can't it? I mean, we learn in the next verse that the whole nation heard what had happened, so if the king had tried the same trick again, the women involved would have said to themselves, 'Ah, it's the old let's-cut-the-baby-in-half ploy.' Both would beg Solomon to give the child to the other rather than killing it. What then?

What if, on this first occasion, both women had given up their claim rather than see the baby harmed? Would he have tossed a shekel and awarded the prize to the winner?

What if neither woman had really cared about the welfare of the child and both had agreed with the decision to cut the poor little thing in half? Not so tricky, that one. Presumably Solomon would have given the baby to someone else altogether.

What if—I've started so I'll finish—the real mother had agreed to the gory division and the other had abandoned her false claim out of compassion for the child? Again, not so difficult. You give the baby to the non-mother on the grounds that the real one has forfeited her rights.

What if… Enough!

Real life presents us with a succession of 'What if…?'s. One thing is for sure, dealing with it requires the wisdom of Solomon. He, of course, got his from God and so, amazingly, can we.

Prayer

Father, the simplest decisions can be challenging. Clear our minds, give us wisdom.

AP

He was an artist and a scholar

God gave Solomon wisdom and very great insight, and a breadth of understanding as measureless as the sand on the seashore. Solomon's wisdom was greater than the wisdom of all the men of the East, and greater than all the wisdom of Egypt. He was wiser than any other man, including Ethan the Ezrahite—wiser than Heman, Calcol and Darda, the sons of Mahol. And his fame spread to all the surrounding nations. He spoke 3000 proverbs and his songs numbered 1005. He described plant life, from the cedar of Lebanon to the hyssop that grows out of walls. He also taught about animals and birds, reptiles and fish. Men of all nations came to listen to Solomon's wisdom, sent by all the kings of the world, who had heard of his wisdom.

Pretty impressive, eh? Philosopher, poet, musician, botanist, zoologist and teacher. Ladies and gentlemen, the next competitor on *Mastermind* is King Solomon, specialist subject—everything!

Given this vast range of interests and absorptions I suppose the king might have selected almost any area in which to direct most of his energies. In fact, predictably perhaps, he decided to concentrate on the temple that his father had never been able to build in his lifetime. Conditions for such a project were excellent. The nation was rich and well-organized. Potential troublemakers had all been removed. There was peace and stability in the land. It was time to honour God by creating an earthly dwelling-place that would surpass anything seen before.

There is no doubt—as we shall see if we take the trouble to read through the detail of the following three chapters—that all the arts and abilities and interests of the king fed into the planning and construction of what must have been a truly magnificent piece of work. I imagine he was a very hands-on project co-ordinator!

There are those who argue that we have nothing to offer God and, of course, they are right in the sense that God is the true author of all things. Having humbly acknowledged that fact, though, we must not be afraid to pour all that we are into the work we do for him. Solomon did.

Prayer

I offer you everything that I am, Lord. Take it and use it.

AP

38

He could get other people on his side

'You know that because of the wars waged against my father David from all sides, he could not build a temple for the Name of the Lord his God until the Lord put his enemies under his feet. But now the Lord my God has given me rest on every side, and there is no adversary or disaster. I intend, therefore, to build a temple for the Name of the Lord my God, as the Lord told my father David, when he said, "Your son whom I will put on the throne in your place will build the temple for my Name." So give orders that cedars of Lebanon will be cut for me. My men will work with yours, and I will pay you for your men whatever wages you set. You know that we have no one as skilled in felling timber as the Sidonians.'

This is Solomon's message to Hiram King of Tyre and if you read on you will see that Hiram produced a very pleased response. You can see why.

First, Solomon does Hiram the courtesy of explaining the context of his request. David was unable to build the temple, but now there is peace and stability enough to begin this huge project. The principle of inclusion holds good in all situations (including DIY stores, I have discovered). Let people into your plans and they might travel with you.

Second, he did not attempt to prescribe or set a wage limit for the workers that would join Hiram's men. Open-endedness in matters of finance has a genuinely liberating effect on relationships, whereas meanness and that awful narrow-eyed wariness that we see so often in our society has exactly the opposite effect. I'm not talking about being silly or irresponsible with money. We are called to be good stewards, but good stewardship sometimes demands an extravagant vulnerability that reflects the very heart of God.

Third, Solomon includes a simply expressed acknowledgement of the special timber-felling skills that the Sidonians are able to offer. Finding that our particular strengths or skills are genuinely appreciated always lifts us and makes us even more able.

Respect, generosity and appreciation. He was no fool, this Solomon, was he?

Prayer

Help us to win the goodwill of others with the tools of grace.

AP

His priorities may have been confused

It took Solomon 13 years, however, to complete the construction of his palace. He built the Palace of the Forest of Lebanon 100 cubits long, 50 wide and 30 high, with 4 rows of cedar columns supporting trimmed cedar beams. It was roofed with cedar above the beams that rested on the columns—45 beams, 15 to a row. Its windows were placed high in sets of three, facing each other... When the queen of Sheba saw all the wisdom of Solomon and the palace he had built, the food on his table, the seating of his officials, the attending servants in their robes, his cupbearers, and the burnt offerings he made at the temple of the Lord, she was overwhelmed. She said to the king, 'The report I heard in my own country about your achievements and your wisdom is true.'

A very simple piece of mathematics for you here. How long did it take for the temple to be built? Seven years is the answer. How long did it take for the king's palace to be built? This time, the answer is thirteen years. Take seven away from thirteen and you are left with six. Six more years were given to the construction of the king's residence than to God's house. That's a long time. Did Solomon get a bit carried away? Is it possible that all the power and the wealth and the admiration went to his head without him even being properly aware of it? What was the effect of being visited by such celebrities as the Queen of Sheba and finding himself and his possessions so openly and fulsomely admired? Note that, quite soon after this visit is recorded, there is a description of the great throne that Solomon had constructed for himself, inlaid with ivory and overlaid with fine gold. Nothing like it, we read (10:18–20), had ever been made for any other kingdom. He soaked himself in splendour.

We know that Solomon was a man of prayer and a follower of the true God, but he was neither the first nor the last to be seduced from the path of pure virtue by things that are tempting but ultimately worthless.

Sunday reflection

Lord, preserve those with leading roles in the Church from the folly of believing their own publicity and being drawn aside by glittering trifles.

AP

He appreciated the mystery of God

The trumpeters and singers joined in unison as with one voice, to give praise and thanks to the Lord. Accompanied by trumpets, cymbals and other instruments, they raised their voices in praise to the Lord and sang: 'He is good; his love endures for ever.' Then the temple of the Lord was filled with a cloud, and the priests could not perform their service because of the cloud, for the glory of the Lord filled the temple of God. Then Solomon said, 'The Lord has said that he would dwell in a dark cloud.'

This is one of my favourite moments in the Old Testament and there are fascinating ideas to be drawn from it. Today, though, I was reflecting on something said by a bishop on television the day before yesterday. I only caught the tail-end of his comments, but it was something about the way in which a desire for immediacy and informality can rob us of an appreciation of the mystery and grandeur of God. It is a difficult tension to maintain, isn't it? We all need the close, uncomplicated love of our heavenly father, the father we are allowed to call 'daddy'. There was a divine ordinariness about the ways of Jesus with vulnerable human beings that, thank God, warms and reassures my heart. The bishop is right, though. In this life we are only able to touch the outermost rim of the farthest edge of the garments of the glory of God. The mystery and splendour of the creator of the universe is as real and as rich as those aspects of him that we do seem to understand.

Here is Solomon, fully in control because he knows that God is as likely to dwell in a dark and mysterious cloud as he is to inhabit the most beautiful dwelling-place constructed by the hands of man.

A small, trusting child confidently clutches his daddy's hand, despite understanding nothing of the big, mysterious world where his father operates. That little world within a much greater universe is all he needs for now. It is a perfectly safe place and how exciting, inspirational and informative it can be to peep out at the mystery and the splendour from a place where no one can hurt the most important part of you.

Prayer
We trust you, Father.

AP

He had a sense of history and destiny

'My father David had it in his heart to build a temple for the Name of the Lord, the God of Israel. But the Lord said to my father David, "Because it was in your heart to build a temple for my Name, you did well to have this in your heart. Nevertheless, you are not the one to build the temple, but your son, who is your own flesh and blood—he is the one who will build the temple for my Name." The Lord has kept the promise he made: I have succeeded David my father and now I sit on the throne of Israel, just as the Lord promised, and I have built the temple for the Name of the Lord, the God of Israel. I have provided a place there for the ark, in which is the covenant of the Lord that he made with our fathers when he brought them out of Egypt.'

Given half a chance, I start raving on about metaphorical pendulums and that's what I'm going to do now. There is a serious danger of moving too far in the direction of immediacy and total clarity (don't make me laugh!) in spiritual matters. In some groups and congregations there is a fear that acknowledgement of history and tradition in some way impedes the work of the Holy Spirit. We only need to stop and think clearly for a moment to see that this is nonsense. Jesus himself was at great pains to place himself and his ministry in the context of God's dealings with men and women over the centuries. Also, it would be foolish and ungrateful of us to forget the heroes of faith who have toiled through the years to build the spiritual platforms that we caper about on nowadays.

Let's be aware of our past. Let's understand how the love of God has landed us in this place at this time. Let's enjoy our various traditions and allow them to enrich experiences of the living God who has been present and working in every phase of our history.

Here is Solomon doing exactly that and what a satisfaction one senses in his awareness of the way in which his very special 'today' completes the jigsaw puzzle of the past.

Prayer

Thank you, Lord, for past, present and future.

AP

He recognized physical and human limits

'But will God really dwell on earth? The heavens, even the highest heaven, cannot contain you. How much less this temple I have built! Yet give attention to your servant's prayer and his plea for mercy, O Lord my God. Hear the cry and the prayer that your servant is praying in your presence this day. May your eyes be open towards this temple night and day, this place of which you have said, "My Name shall be there," so that you will hear the prayer your servant prays towards this place... When they sin against you—for there is no one who does not sin—and you become angry with them and give them over to the enemy, who takes them captive to his own land, far away or near... And forgive your people.'

Do read the whole prayer (8:23–53). It is fascinating to see how this realistic king seeks to cover all possible contingencies in his nation's life. He has few blind spots about things or people.

It took Solomon seven years to build that temple, every tiny detail crucially important to him. It was to be an ideal dwelling-place for the creator, the greatest architectural feat in history. Nevertheless, the king acknowledges that God is too vast to be contained within the finest building. He pleads with God, though, to let his eyes be open towards the temple, so that the king's prayers will be heard.

Similarly, he is clear-eyed about human beings. Solomon is not addressing some hypothetical situation in which the people of Israel might sin. He knows that no one can avoid sin and he is pleading in advance for forgiveness and return from exile if that is to be the nation's punishment.

Good lessons.

You may spend millions on church buildings. Some are doing exactly that. Those places will not contain God, nor persuade him to be any more present than when he is invited into the single room of a praying pensioner who can no longer leave home.

As for the problem of sin, well, like the poor, it is always with us and that realization should encourage us to be very, very gentle with each other. The temple of the Holy Spirit is being built and rebuilt daily within each one of us.

Prayer
Dwell in me, a sinner.

AP

He was not insular in his thinking

'As for the foreigner who does not belong to your people Israel but has come from a distant land because of your great name and your mighty hand and your outstretched arm—when he comes and prays towards this temple, then hear from heaven, your dwelling-place, and do whatever the foreigner asks of you, so that all the peoples of the earth may know your name and fear you, as do your own people Israel, and may know that this house that I have built bears your Name. When your people go to war against their enemies, wherever you send them, and when they pray to you towards this city you have chosen and the temple I have built for your Name, then hear from heaven their prayer and their plea, and uphold their cause.'

Here is another extract from Solomon's great prayer of dedication, offered before the whole assembly of the people. Perhaps it constitutes a message to them as much as a request to God. The second part of the passage—a prayer that God will uphold the king's army when it is away at war—would have been familiar to those who were listening. Of course it was to be hoped that the righteous pleas of their troops would be heard and granted. The first part, however, is a declaration to all who are present that the God of Israel is likely to listen to the prayers of outsiders, to those who have seen and appreciated the goodness of the Lord and wish to throw themselves on his mercy. The welcoming of strangers was already traditional in Israel, but this was a plea from Solomon that the whole world should come to know and worship the one true God.

How sad to contrast the wide-armed spiritual optimism of this prayer and attitude with the scrunched-up little prejudices that we continue to suffer from in some sections of the modern Church. Even within the Christian faith itself, there are denominations that refuse to have contact with other denominations, let alone with strangers to the faith. How have we allowed this to happen? May the Lord send us leaders who will throw their arms wide like Solomon and pray strangers into the kingdom of God.

Prayer
Send them, Lord!

AP

2 Chronicles 7:11–16 (NIV, abridged)

He was assured of God's presence in the temple

When Solomon had finished the temple... the Lord appeared to him at night and said: 'I have heard your prayer and have chosen this place for myself as a temple for sacrifices. When I shut up the heavens so that there is no rain, or command locusts to devour the land or send a plague among my people, if my people, who are called by my name, will humble themselves and pray and seek my face and turn from their wicked ways, then will I hear from heaven and will forgive their sin and will heal their land. Now my eyes will be open and my ears attentive to the prayers offered in this place. I have chosen and consecrated this temple so that my Name may be there for ever. My eyes and my heart will always be there.'

We don't build temples out of wood and brick and stone any more, do we? Instead, the Bible tells us, we are temples (1 Corinthians 6:19). Each one of us can be a place where God lives. Bearing this in mind, you may find it interesting to read this passage again, as I've just done, and see how it applies as an assurance from God to us as individual Christians.

A few weeks ago, Bridget and I hosted an evening on behalf of the Kenward Trust, a Christian organization that offers light at the end of the long dark tunnel of drug and alcohol misuse. It was a highly inspiring evening for us, quite apart from anyone in the audience. Two of the men who have been helped by a residential placement at one of the Kenward houses were up on the stage answering questions about the past, the present and, thank God, the future. Certainly a plague had passed across the lives of these two people, but now they were following Jesus and the healing process was well under way. I am quite sure that God's eyes and ears are open and attentive to the prayers that they offer. Our prayer for them is that his name will be on their lips for the rest of their days.

Prayer

Father, you are building temples all over the world. May they remain strong and beautiful and may your eyes and heart be always with them.

AP

He could not resist the wrong women

King Solomon, however, loved many foreign women besides Pharaoh's daughter—Moabites, Ammonites, Edomites, Sidonians and Hittites. They were from nations about which the Lord had told the Israelites, 'You must not intermarry with them, because they will surely turn your hearts after their gods.' Nevertheless, Solomon held fast to them in love. He had 700 wives of royal birth and 300 concubines, and his wives led him astray. As Solomon grew old, his wives turned his heart after other gods, and his heart was not fully devoted to the Lord his God, as the heart of David his father had been... The Lord became angry with Solomon because his heart had turned away from the Lord, the God of Israel, who had appeared to him twice.

(If you can, read the whole of chapter 11.) Oh dear, he was his father's son. As well as inheriting many fine characteristics, Solomon seems to have ended up with one of David's major weaknesses.

Years earlier, on a spring night in the battle season, another king had paced the palace walls, wondering how the battle was going and wishing he was there (2 Samuel 11). He had spied the beautiful figure of Bathsheba, Solomon's mother, and seduced her. In this, and in concealing his adultery with the murder of Uriah, her husband, he had greatly angered God. God forgave David, but his punishment was the dire calamity that came upon him from his own household. David had never worshipped false gods, but sheer lust started trouble in his life.

Solomon fell for the same reason. There's no fool like an old fool, they say and, as Solomon grew elderly, he allowed his foreign wives to seduce him into following the Sidonian Ashtoreth and Molech, the god of the Ammonites. As a result of this treachery, God raised up enemies against him and allowed his son only one tribe of Israel after the king's death.

How could he have done it? How? After all God had given and done for him, how could Solomon, with his riches and his concubines and his hundreds of wives, have been so foolishly wicked as to chase after foreign gods? It beggars belief, but I'm afraid the same sort of thing still happens.

Prayer

Lord, we are weak and easily tempted. Help us to be strong and obedient in your service.

AP

The Holy Spirit

At the beginning of the book of Acts (ch. 2), we read of a large crowd gathered in Jerusalem from all over the known world. Between them they had seen all the ancient wonders of the world, had experienced amazing natural wonders and exciting human 'shows'. They were, however, totally taken aback by the phenomena of the day of Pentecost.

As people always do, they attempted to account for the bizarre events by relating it to their previous experiences. Nothing was sufficient, however, because the phenomena not only had a supernatural origin but also was inaugurating a new era in God's strategy. For this was the Spirit of God, bursting the old wineskins! The only way to truly appreciate it was by reference to the prophecy of Joel (Acts 2:17). Thus, Peter challenged the crowd to recognize that, as a consequence of the death and resurrection of Jesus, the last days—the last days of the Spirit—had come.

In the light of this prophecy, an exciting time lay ahead for those who would believe that Jesus was God's Messiah. Here was a radical universalizing and intensifying of the impact of the Holy Spirit. No longer was he restricted to prophets, priests and kings, but even the servants had their share. No longer was he to confine his operations to one generation, but young or old could equally be channels of his blessing. Gender issues, too, dissolved into insignificance. Here is encouragement for each of us to explore and appropriate the 'ministry of the Holy Spirit', whoever we may be.

While this prophecy from Joel was critical to understanding the events of Pentecost, the coming of God's Spirit was not the fulfilling of one prophecy alone. The Holy Spirit's footsteps can be seen in many places throughout the Old Testament. In these readings we are intentionally paralleling Old Testament glimpses of the Spirit with the fuller revelation that the coming of Jesus makes possible. It is certainly true that the New Testament provides us with immeasurably more insight into the life and ministry of the Holy Spirit than the Old Testament does (as it also does for the life and ministry of the Messiah!) However, I believe that by including some Old Testament insights, our reading of the New and our involvement with God's Holy Spirit will be enriched. So, I invite you to join me on this journey of discovery.

David Spriggs

47

The Spirit and creation

In the beginning God created the heavens and the earth. The earth was barren with no form of life; it was under a roaring ocean covered with darkness. But the Spirit of God was moving over the water. God said, 'I command light to shine!' And light started shining.

Do you find TV programmes of the likes of *Horizon* both fascinating and sometimes frightening? When they allow us to gaze into distant parts of the universe and see not only millions of stars but also millions of galaxies, each with millions of stars, it is awesome. When we learn that the larger part of all the energy in the universe is 'dark matter' and 'dark energy' that scientists know must be there but cannot observe, even with all their amazing technology, it becomes overwhelming. I have the same experience when I try to think about the light of the stars that I can see today actually having been emitted from them millions of years ago. Also, when I try to imagine the vastness of space, I inwardly collapse!

Until, that is, I recall that this is God's universe and the fact that we can even begin to grasp the enormity of our world says something about us. The fact that it is understandable at all tells us how remarkable it is not only for its complexity, but also in some ways for its simplicity and certainly for its beauty.

The way those who first heard Genesis 1:1–3 saw the universe, is, in one sense, very different from how we see it today, but fundamentally they were like us—aware of its vastness, otherness and power. It seemed unreachable and uncontrollable, but their faith told them something else, something more profound and more important for people—this strange universe was God's creation and their own lives were his gift. Even before creation, written into the fabric of existence itself, even the apparently unimaginable chaos (the roaring ocean) was within God's purposes. They expressed this by saying, 'But the Spirit of God was moving over the water.'

Those wonderful words state that the most significant point about the universe is that it is shaped by the purposes and power of God. God's Spirit is waiting his moment and his time.

Sunday reflection
I believe in God the Father, maker of heaven and earth...

DS

JOHN 3:5–8a (CEV)

The Spirit and new creation

Jesus answered: 'I tell you for certain that before you can get into God's kingdom, you must be born not only by water but by the Spirit. Humans give life to their children. Yet only God's Spirit can change you into a child of God. Don't be surprised when I say that you must be born from above. Only God's Spirit gives new life. The Spirit is like the wind that blows wherever it wants to....'

There is another universe and another chaos: the chaos of our human minds. Discovering something of the inner workings of the mind can also be a frightening experience. When we learn that our choices can easily be manipulated by advertising gurus who understand our subconscious drives or that our most rational thinking and argument is shaped by our need for power, it is disturbing enough. However, when we come face to face with our own evil, where can we go for we cannot escape ourselves? Are we forever captives of our own genes, victims of our past experiences or caged by our previous choices?

According to Jesus, there is hope, because we can be 'born again' or, more precisely, 'born from above'. There is hope because, just as we have experienced a natural human birth (literally 'out of water', which I take to refer to the water surrounding the foetus in the womb), so there is the possibility of a birth of a different kind of order—of the Spirit.

Before this possibility can become a reality, we have to face two hard facts. First, we cannot become a new kind of person (any more than we engineered our own birth!) by our own effort, even when that effort is informed by scriptural insights, as was certainly the case for Nicodemus. Second, we cannot control the process—it can only happen when God's Holy Spirit is in charge (see v. 8). In fact, this new birth is only possible because Jesus is given by the Father and that 'giving' includes his death on the cross (vv. 13–15).

Reflection

Can you share God's hope of new birth as Jesus did with Nicodemus? Perhaps you know someone who is seeking to understand their identity, discover a way out of their chaos or make sense of life after failure or disappointment.

DS

The Spirit as God's mark of power

All the Midianites, Amalekites, and other eastern nations got together and crossed the River Jordan. Then they invaded the land of Israel and set up camp in Jezreel Valley. The Lord's Spirit took control of Gideon, and Gideon blew a signal on a trumpet to tell the men in the Abiezer clan to follow him. He also sent messengers to the tribes of Manasseh, Asher, Zebulun, and Naphtali, telling the men of these tribes to come and join his army. Then they set out towards the enemy camp.

How can a fearful, diffident young man become a courageous and confident leader? This is certainly what happened to Gideon. When we first meet him, he is hiding in the wine press from the national enemy, the Midianites. As we find him here (vv. 34–35), he is a decisive leader, although his natural timidity still shows through (vv. 39–40).

The change in character, or at least performance, is explained in the words, 'The Lord's Spirit took control of Gideon'. We can see three outcomes from this. First, he blew a trumpet: that is, he acted boldly and decisively. This trumpet was clearly a recognized sign to rally the tribe. He must have seen the danger of the invasion and the opportunity of the moment. Second, he sent out messengers to raise the fighting forces of four other tribes: his empowerment by God's Spirit gave him validity beyond the narrow confines of his own group. We can also see wisdom in this act, in that he knew that he needed more forces than his clan could provide and so appealed to the tribal bonding. Third, the Spirit of God led him to seek confirmation from God before he acted. The following chapter, which narrates how the invasion was defeated, is also marked by Gideon's willingness to listen to God and obey him.

Boldness, wisdom and an increased intensity of relationship with God are three characteristics of God's Spirit taking control of a person.

(For the full story, read Judges 6:1—7:25.)

Reflection

Think of situations where Christians need to show courage today and pray for them. Pray for people, including yourself, who would benefit from allowing God's Spirit to produce these qualities in them. Pray, too, for Christians who face severe opposition because of their faith.

DS

The Spirit as God's mark of ownership

Christ also brought you the truth, which is the good news about how you can be saved. You put your faith in Christ and were given the promised Holy Spirit to show that you belong to God. The Spirit also makes us sure that we will be given what God has stored up for his people. Then we will be set free, and God will be honoured and praised.

Gideon was amazed when the angel addressed him as a 'strong warrior' (Judges 6:12). It was equally amazing that Gentiles should receive a full welcome into God's household (Ephesians 2:19–22). For Paul, one of the incontrovertible indicators for this was that Gentiles had been given the Holy Spirit: 'You put your faith in Christ and were given the promised Holy Spirit' (2:13). Paul uses many evocative pictures to explain the significance of God's Spirit. We will explore one of those mentioned here—that God's Spirit is a seal.

The Holy Spirit is God's seal, 'to show that you belong to God' (v. 13). Trade was very important in Asia Minor, but, without trading standards officers, how could you know that the wine or olive oil you bought was of the proper standard and how could you really know where it had come from? The solution was that flagons of wine or casks of oil would be marked with a wax seal. If this was unbroken, it guaranteed that the contents had not been tampered with. Moreover, it also told you who had produced the wine or oil. This personal mark was important in days when travel was much slower than today. It also meant that, if you had a problem, you knew where to go to sort things out.

Furthermore the originator's mark ensured that the quality would be high, for they had associated their reputation with the goods. It didn't matter if the container was dusty or battered by the long journey, as it was what was inside that really mattered. In the same way, Paul recognized that even if people were slaves, ex-prostitutes or personnel from the Temple of Aphrodite, if they had received God's Spirit then God was guaranteeing the quality of the person, for ultimately they belonged to him.

Prayer

Lord, help me, through your Spirit, to know that I am precious to you.

DS

The Spirit and social transformation

Like a branch that sprouts from a stump, someone from David's family will some day be king. The Spirit of the Lord will be with him to give him understanding, wisdom, and insight. He will be powerful and he will know and honour the Lord. His greatest joy will be to obey the Lord…. The poor and the needy will be treated with fairness…. Leopards will lie down with young goats… Just as water fills the sea, the land will be filled with people who know and honour the Lord.

Think back to the death of the Queen Mother. It was quite remarkable how many people, young as well as old, were prepared to queue for hours to walk past her coffin or see it pass by them on its way to Westminster Abbey. Whether it was respect for her, a sense of history or identification with national sorrow, all indicate the recognition of the significance of the monarchy, even in our parliamentary democracy.

For Israel, the kind of king you had was far more fundamental: law and governance, peace and prosperity, worship and divine favour all depended on the king. That is why the book of Kings evaluates each reign from the standpoint of the monarchy's relationship with God. Sadly the people often suffered the consequences of the weak character or selfish intent of their king. Sometimes this resulted in personal injustice, sometimes internal strife and bloodshed; sometimes it meant devastation from an external aggressor, such as Assyria, or even exile, with the resultant loss of identity for individuals and the nation. The king mattered to everyone!

So it was that, appreciating both the importance of the king and the weaknesses of every human leader, this prophecy in Isaiah looks to a time when 'the Spirit of the Lord' will ensure that the king is wise, just and strong. The results will be justice for the poor, peace (even between animals), prosperity and a sense of God's presence penetrating every part of society. The enrichment of the king's life with the Spirit of God brings not only divine characteristics to him, but life-enhancing blessing to all and a real awareness of God's presence.

(For further reading, see the whole passage of Isaiah 11:1–9.)

Prayer

For all who govern, that God's Spirit will be able to work through them.

DS

The Spirit and personal transformation

If you are guided by the Spirit, you won't obey your selfish desires… God's Spirit makes us loving, happy, peaceful, patient, kind, good, faithful, gentle, and self-controlled. There is no law against behaving in any of these ways. And because we belong to Christ Jesus, we have killed our selfish feelings and desires. God's Spirit has given us life, and so we should follow the Spirit. But don't be conceited or make others jealous by claiming to be better than they are.

Isaiah's dream was of a divinely inspired king who would bring the characteristics of God's life into every aspect of the nation. Paul's dream is even more breathtaking, but, to be fair, it was based on what had been seen of God in Jesus. He did have something of an advantage over Isaiah in that respect!

How everyone longs always to be treated lovingly and patiently, with kindness, gentleness and reliability! This, says Paul, is how people who have been transformed by the Holy Spirit behave. Look at the 'body, mind, spirit' section in a bookshop or watch a few TV programmes and you can soon see that most people would love to be happy, peaceful and self-controlled. Yet these are the changes that happen when God's Spirit is in control of anyone's life. Paul knew this because, as has often been pointed out, the 'fruit of the Spirit' reads like a snapshot of the character of Jesus in the Gospels. The Holy Spirit is someone who does for us now what Jesus did then.

In what way is Paul's dream more breathtaking than Isaiah's? It is partly his description of the richness and depth of character that the Spirit brings, but mainly it is because he tells how the Spirit's transforming work is not restricted to the king but is the birthright of every believer. However, a birthright can be squandered, as Esau did (Genesis 25:27–34), so it needs not only to be claimed, but also lived out responsibly. This is our part, making space for God's Spirit and being willing for him to do his work in us.

Reflection

Look carefully at the qualities the Spirit brings. Thank God for everyone in whom you see these features. Try to think of at least one Christian for each of them, then ask God to make you more like Jesus through his Spirit.

DS

The Spirit and Isaiah's servanthood

Here is my servant! I have made him strong. He is my chosen one; I am pleased with him. I have given him my Spirit, and he will bring justice to the nations. He won't shout or yell or call out in the streets. He won't break off a bent reed or put out a dying flame, but he will make sure that justice is done. He won't stop or give up until he brings justice everywhere on earth.

God's Spirit represents his transforming presence, operating within the sphere of the world. We can see this in the account of creation and the way that the Spirit energizes people for tasks that require courage and strength. With this background, it is at first surprising that God says he has given his Spirit to his servant, especially when the servant is described as unattractive, filled with sorrow and despised (Isaiah 53:1–3). So what is going on? Some very exciting transformations in understanding, is the answer!

It is still clear from our passage that the Spirit is a sign of favour ('chosen', 'I am pleased with him') and also that the Spirit, in one way, still produces the same impact ('I have made him strong'), but the style of operating has changed.

True, his task is still to bring justice, re-establish the proper order for human society, but now this is not to be achieved primarily by sending Israel's enemies packing and ensuring stability within her borders, but by endeavouring to bring 'justice to the nations' (v. 1). As we can see from verse 7, this involves 'sight to the blind' and the setting free of prisoners—not so much thieves and murderers as people who have been imprisoned when their countries have been conquered. Moreover, rather than blowing trumpets and issuing rallying cries, the Lord's servant 'won't shout or yell'.

So where is God's power at work? It can be seen in that servant who will not give up (even if it involves death) until people everywhere can have their hunger for divine insight satisfied. He will carry out and complete God's mission.

(For a fuller picture, read 42:1–7; 61:1–7.)

Reflection

How do you picture God's power at work most clearly—in a great earthquake, the destruction of vicious people or the suffering of Christians for their faith?

DS

The Spirit and servanthood

While everyone else was being baptized, Jesus himself was baptized. Then as he prayed, the sky opened up, and the Holy Spirit came down upon him in the form of a dove. A voice from heaven said, 'You are my own dear Son, and I am pleased with you.' ... When Jesus returned from the River Jordan, the power of the Holy Spirit was with him, and the Spirit led him into the desert. For 40 days Jesus was tested by the devil.

The essential nature of Christian leadership is that it is servant leadership. This is the kind of leadership that Jesus chose for himself and it is the kind of leadership that he expects from his followers (John 13:1–20). It is not natural for leaders to behave like this, however, and it is in the nature of the power of leadership to corrupt.

At his baptism, Jesus received the Holy Spirit in a new and intense way. He also received confirmation that his ministry was one of service, which would ultimately lead to his death as a ransom for many (see Mark 10:45 and Philippians 2:1–11). His temptations show Jesus wrestling with and resisting various aspects of non-servant leadership and his sermon in Nazareth (Luke 4:18–27) shows his public declaration and commitment to the servant way. Throughout these episodes, Luke emphasizes the presence of the Spirit with Jesus (see 3:21–22; 4:1, 14, 18), because only with the empowering and sensitizing qualities of God's Spirit will Jesus keep on track. It is a very hard road to stay on.

Each of us leads—in the home if not at work; in the church if not at the WI; in some set of relationships if not as the captain of the team; on odd occasions if not by character. It is so important that we, like Jesus, lead with a servant heart, for it is a critical part of our witness for him. We certainly have no chance of success without the Holy Spirit's indwelling, but neither can we succeed without resisting the corruption that power can bring.

(For further reading, see Luke 4:1–30.)

Sunday reflection

Imagine God sending his Holy Spirit on you like a dove, with all the challenges to lead like Jesus coming with it.

DS

EXODUS 31:1–6 (CEV)

Creative gifts

The Lord said to Moses: 'I have chosen Bezalel from the Judah tribe to make the sacred tent and its furnishings. Not only have I filled him with my Spirit, but I have given him wisdom and made him a skilled craftsman who can create objects of art with gold, silver, bronze, stone and wood. I have appointed Oholiab from the tribe of Dan to work with him.

In terms both of function and space devoted to it, the construction of the 'sacred tent' is clearly of great significance. It is where Moses and Aaron will meet with God and where sacrifices will be offered, enabling the covenant relationship to flourish. It is where Israel's sacred laws will be kept, indicating the centrality of these for her life as well as their divine origins. Above all, it is to be a place of worship, where God can meet his people and they can respond. So, although it is unusual, it is not surprising that the chief craftsman should be filled with God's Spirit—God tells Moses that he has 'filled him with my Spirit' and Moses tells the people the same (Exodus 31:3; 35:31).

As far as I know, Bezalel is the only craftsman to be designated in this way. It is important that creative and artistic skills are associated with God's Spirit. Wisdom, skilled craftsmanship, the ability to create objects of art with gold, silver, bronze, stone and wood are all mentioned, as are design and embroidery. We should celebrate these gifts and their creative achievements as indications of the creativity of God.

We should also recognize, however, that, according to scripture, the gift of God's Spirit is additional to these. Thus, Oholiab is closely associated with Bezalel in all his abilities, but is never said to have received God's Spirit. So the evidence of amazing creativity and artistic ability is not in itself synonymous with having God's Spirit! This is true even when the purpose is as significant a project as constructing the 'sacred tent'. (Nor, for that matter, is the ability to write, even Bible-reading notes, in itself evidence of God's Spirit!)

Prayer

Lord, help us to recognize and celebrate the origins of all creative abilities in you, but give us the discernment to know when these gifts are also flowing directly from your Spirit within us.

DS

Spiritual gifts

There are different kinds of spiritual gifts, but they all come from the same Spirit... The Spirit has given each of us a special way of serving others. Some of us can speak with wisdom, while others can speak with knowledge, but these gifts come from the same Spirit. To others the Spirit has given great faith or the power to heal the sick or the power to perform mighty miracles. Some of us are prophets, and some of us recognize when God's Spirit is present... But it is the Spirit who does all this and decides which gifts to give to each of us.

When we come to the New Testament, the range of people gifted with the Spirit, as well as the gifts themselves, suddenly opens out—rather than a river in a narrow channel, it now spreads out across the whole land (see Ezekiel 47:1–12; Revelation 22:1–2). Paul emphasizes that the variety of gifts is evidence of the richness of the nature of God (see vv. 4–11). Every believer has been given some gift (v. 7). Now the gifts are not primarily for building a place of worship, but to facilitate the construction of worship itself. So gifts such as wisdom, knowledge, preaching, prophesying and speaking in tongues ('different kinds of languages', v. 10) are mentioned, as well as performing miracles and healing the sick. The way in which these are to be evaluated, according to Paul, is the extent to which they help to build up the congregation (see 14:12, for instance). In line with this is how Paul indicates gifts such as speaking in tongues should be used. They are to be used in ways that facilitate the worship of the congregation and not merely to exalt the person with the gift; they are not for show but to show the reality of God within the gathered community.

How many gifts of the Spirit can you recognize being used in your worship services? Are you aware of the gifts of the Spirit that God has given to you? Are you able to rejoice in the richness of gifts that God has given to people in your church?

Prayer

Holy Spirit of God, help me to know if there are spiritual gifts that I find difficult to welcome. Help me to understand why this may be.

DS

Community-building: covenant renewed

I will wash away everything that makes you unclean, and I will remove your disgusting idols. I will take away your stubborn heart and give you a new heart and a desire to be faithful. You will have only pure thoughts, because I will put my Spirit in you and make you eager to obey my laws and teachings. You will once again live in the land I gave your ancestors; you will be my people, and I will be your God.

Yesterday's passage emphasized the importance of the Spirit for the worship of the community of God's people. Today's brings out an even more fundamental role of the Spirit within the life of God's people: only the Spirit can ensure the viability of the covenant people.

There is irony in this passage. God's punishment of Israel in the form of their exile to Babylon was intended to establish the holiness of God—Israel's blatant sins (murder and idolatry) had to be overtly punished. Rather than leading the Babylonians to recognize God's holiness, however, it had led to disgrace. They were saying that God had driven Israel out, turned against them and forsaken them (vv. 17–22). So God intends, even though they do not deserve it, to restore them to their land, re-establish his integrity. How can he do this and remain holy?

The pivotal answer is by means of his Spirit. All kinds of exciting promises precede this, such as bringing them home, cleansing them to make them acceptable to God, as well as removing their idols (vv. 24–25). All kinds of exhilarating promises follow, too, including ongoing protection from uncleanness, unprecedented prosperity, restoration of their towns and answered prayers (vv. 29–38), but at the core is the promise 'I will put my Spirit in you' (v. 27). He will make them eager to obey God's laws, they will have a new heart and so desire to be faithful. God will enable the covenant to be re-established and, with it, their identity and community: 'you will be my people, and I will be your God' (v. 28).

(If you have time, please read Jeremiah 31:31–34 and especially Ezekiel 36:17–38.)

Reflection

What does this passage have to say to a declining Church? Does it have anything to say to us as a nation?

DS

Community-building: covenant established

You Gentiles are no longer strangers and foreigners.... You are like a building with the apostles and prophets as the foundation and with Christ as the most important stone. Christ is the one who holds the building together and makes it grow into a holy temple for the Lord. And you are part of that building Christ has built as a place for God's own Spirit to live.

Paul never ceased to be amazed at the miracle of the death and resurrection of Jesus. Those who were enemies of God and dead to divine life, dead to their own destiny as people made in God's image and those who were intractable enemies of one another (the Jews and the Gentiles) had all been united as the people of God. Paul even dared to say that the Gentiles are part of the 'temple' along with the Jews. The temple was the most important place on earth for it was the place where heaven intersected with earth, being a symbol (perhaps we should say 'sacrament') of the place where God resides and makes his presence available. Paul knew the Gentiles were an integral part of God's new 'temple' because the Spirit of God lived among them too and there is only one Spirit (4:4).

This has moral and personal consequences. The Spirit of God is able to change the kinds of people we are and the ways we think and act, even as Ezekiel had predicted (see yesterday's reading). However, this only happens as we allow God's Spirit to operate in us. Hence, Paul writes, 'Try your best to let God's Spirit...' and 'Let the Spirit change your way of thinking...' (4:3 and 23). We are more involved than Ezekiel indicated as it takes effort to be humble, gentle and patient; it requires discipline to stop stealing, using dirty talk and cursing each other, if these have been our normal ways of living. However, if in this sense it's harder than Ezekiel thought, in another sense it is easier to know what pleasing God and being holy really means, for we have the life of Jesus as our focus and stimulus.

(Please read 4:3–4, 23–24, if you can.)

Prayer

Holy Spirit, do for us what we cannot and help us to be willing to let you.

DS

59

The Spirit and mission

The Spirit of the Lord God has taken control of me! The Lord has chosen and sent me to tell the oppressed the good news, to heal the brokenhearted, and to announce freedom for prisoners and captives. This is the year when the Lord God will show kindness to us and punish our enemies.

For all their familiarity, these verses still sound like a fanfare, demanding our attention and stirring hope in our hearts. They are even more startling because they are a personal claim, not one made to someone else. These verses tell of God's Spirit doing something new, although in one sense it is something old.

'Taking control' of someone is also the way the book of Judges (3:10; 6:34) describes the energizing intervention of God that enabled charismatic leaders to throw off the cruel domination of foreign tribes; yet here, in the context of exile and spiritual desolation, it is startlingly new.

Being 'chosen' by the Lord was what the coming of the Spirit indicated, but it also promised victory and favour. It became the word for Israel's king. Now that the monarchy was a forgotten reality or at best a historical reminiscence, to claim it as a present experience was revolutionary. The really startling claim was the purpose of the Spirit's coming—not primarily to destroy the enemy, but to commission a messenger to bring good news to the powerless and marginalized.

Here we see clearly the connection of God's Spirit with gospel mission, but there are two ways in which this amazing passage falls short of the New Testament's reality. First, the consequence of the realized hope for the oppressed is the destruction of Israel's enemies. Second, the focus of this outpouring of blessing is Jerusalem, not the whole world. True, foreigners do find a place, but only as hired labour, while the people of God become honoured as priests of God who receive all the treasures of the nations as tribute! Nevertheless, the fact that Jesus chose this passage to announce his ministry (Luke 4:18–19) suggests that we should value this passage very highly.

Meditation

Give yourself a spiritual check-up. Does your attitude to other people, groups and nations reflect the fuller revelation of the Spirit that Jesus gives?

DS

The Spirit and our mission

While he [Jesus] was still with them, he said: 'Don't leave Jerusalem yet. Wait here for the Father to give you the Holy Spirit, just as I told you he has promised to do... the Holy Spirit will come upon you and give you power. Then you will tell everyone about me in Jerusalem, in all Judea, in Samaria, and everywhere in the world.' ... On the day of Pentecost all the Lord's followers were together in one place.

So the waiting was over and the time to move forward with the gospel of Jesus Christ had come. I try and imagine how those twelve disciples and the women with them would have felt.

Were they relieved that the waiting Jesus had prescribed was now over, as indeed was the perplexity about what exactly would happen when 'the Spirit comes upon you' and how they would know it had taken place. Were they even more confused by the outcome with so many people from so many cultures clamouring to join the Christian community (read on in chapter 2). The 120 believers were joined by another 5000. How would they cope with making them disciples? Surely there was no energy left to cope with expansion?

Were they excited beyond words as they experienced the 'greater things' that Jesus had promised would accompany the Spirit's coming? Were they fearful that such a movement of people into the Christian community, with all the ramifications for the Jewish leaders, would soon bring disaster on them?

I can only imagine how, had I had been one of them, all these reactions would have swept over me many times during those early days after Pentecost. One thing I would have known for sure, though —life could never be the same. God had pulled the cork out of the bottle and there was no way to get it back in again.

There is no way back. If we are impelled by the Holy Spirit, the Spirit of Jesus, we can only go forward, taking his offer of forgiveness, purpose, new identity, power to live by and hope to die for with us to share with all.

Meditation

Should we translate 'in Jerusalem, in all Judea, in Samaria, and everywhere in the world' (1:8) as family, friends, workmates and everyone with whom we have contact?

DS

Belief on trial

The next fortnight's readings are about people's faith under pressure, faith wavering, faith faltering. Most of us will have little difficulty identifying with their problems. The fascinating thing is that almost all of them are people of faith, whom God subsequently used to fulfil wonderful things or bear witness to him in a challenging way. What their stories tell us is that doubt, hesitation, even downright cowardice in the face of the enemy, do not automatically disqualify people from standing in the ranks of the heroes and heroines of the faith.

The examples come from almost every part of the Bible. They include patriarchs (and a patriarch's wife), prophets, generals and kings. They also include a disillusioned husband and wife trudging home, their hopes and dreams shattered. Among them are an anonymous father of a sick boy, a woman near the tomb of her beloved brother, two apostles and an elder in the Church who demurred at being asked to present himself at the house where a notorious scourge of believers was staying. The list ends with another anonymous man, an African, whose search for truth and God reached its climax when he cried out for help—and got it at the side of a desert road!

These stories are a healthy antidote to the common fear of Christians that 'my faith isn't strong enough'. No one can artificially inflate faith, like pumping up a tyre. We can't make ourselves believe. Anyway, that isn't necessary—when Jesus' disciples asked him to 'increase' their faith, he told them that faith 'the size of a mustard seed' would do (Luke 17:5–6). It's not how big the faith is, but how big is the One in whom we place that faith. A little faith in a big God is infinitely better than big faith in a little one!

These stories also tell us that doubt isn't the opposite of faith—that is, unbelief. The people in these stories believed, but at crucial moments that genuine faith was stretched to breaking point. It can happen to any of us. It has certainly happened to me. However, it is at those moments, as the experiences of these people tell us, that our faithful God stands firm. The apostle Paul puts it in a neat paradox: 'If we are faithless, he remains faithful—for he cannot deny himself' (2 Timothy 2:13).

David Winter

GENESIS 3:1–5 (NRSV)

Did God say?

Now the serpent was more crafty than any other wild animal that the Lord God had made. He said to the woman, 'Did God say, "You shall not eat from any tree in the garden"?' The woman said to the serpent, 'We may eat of the fruit of the trees in the garden; but God said, "You shall not eat of the fruit of the tree that is in the middle of the garden, nor shall you touch it, or you shall die."' But the serpent said to the woman, 'You will not die; for God knows that when you eat of it your eyes will be opened, and you will be like God, knowing good and evil.'

This is part of the story of the temptation in the Garden of Eden. Having set the man and the woman in this garden of delights, God gives them one simple command. They may eat anything in the garden (which is overflowing with delicious fruit), but not the fruit of the tree in the middle of the garden. Of course, that becomes the one tree the fruit of which they desperately want to taste!

However, we read the story (and to me it has all the hallmarks of brilliant allegory), we can recognize the truth that lies behind it. At the heart of sin lies disobedience and at the heart of disobedience lies the sneaking feeling that we know better than God. The serpent insinuates the idea very neatly: 'Has God said…?' If he has, why, well, it's because he knows the tremendous benefits that would accrue from eating that particular fruit.

The woman fell for it (and so did the man). 'When the woman saw that the tree was good for food, and that it was a delight to the eyes', she took the fruit and ate it, as did her husband (v. 6). It's easy to suggest that the sin was sensuality—taste and sight—but, in fact, the battle was already lost when she began to question if God knew best. That is, surely, the pattern of all sin—to question the wisdom of God; worse, to think that we know better than our creator what is good for us!

Sunday reflection

In our worship today, as we say words of confession or reflect on our need for forgiveness, let's also address the heart of every sin—the pride that thinks we know best!

DW

The fearful hero of faith

Now there was a famine in the land. So Abram went down to Egypt to reside there as an alien, for the famine was severe in the land. When he was about to enter Egypt, he said to his wife Sarai, 'I know well that you are a woman beautiful in appearance; and when the Egyptians see you, they will say, "This is his wife"; then they will kill me, but they will let you live. Say you are my sister, so that it may go well with me because of you, and that my life may be spared on your account.'

Abram (as he was known at this stage) has already proved the strength of his faith by uprooting himself from Ur of the Chaldees and travelling, at the Lord's command, to the land of Canaan. Now, following the outbreak of famine there, he and his wife Sarai (later Sarah) have sought refuge and food in Egypt. The whole story of Abram speaks of faith and courage, but this strange episode—typical in its ruthless honesty about a patriarch—shows him in an uncharacteristic moment of cowardice. Indeed, he risked his wife's life, as well as his own, by this rather despicable tactic of pretending that she was his sister rather than his wife—in effect, inviting Pharaoh, no less, to take her as his wife (12:15).

Although Abram reaped short-term benefits—food, cattle, camels and slaves—Pharaoh's household was visited with a plague as a result of this illicit relationship.

Pharaoh discovered the deception and had both of them thrown out of the country.

It's a miserable picture, reflecting no credit at all on Abram. There's no need to ask why he did it—we're actually told! He was afraid—afraid that his beautiful wife would be so alluring to the Egyptians that they would kill him in order to take her. In other words, he simply did not trust that the God who had brought him from Chaldea and promised him a 'great nation' could actually look after his wife and himself in a foreign land. Even the great heroes of faith exhibit feet of clay sometimes!

Reflection
Sometimes we are at our weakest in those areas of our lives where we think we are strongest.

DW

GENESIS 18:10–15 (NRSV, ABRIDGED)

The laughter of unbelief

Then one [the Lord] said, 'I will surely return to you in due season, and your wife Sarah shall have a son.' And Sarah was listening at the tent entrance behind him. Now Abraham and Sarah were old, advanced in age; it had ceased to be with Sarah after the manner of women. So Sarah laughed to herself, saying, 'After I have grown old, and my husband is old, shall I have pleasure?' The Lord said to Abraham, 'Why did Sarah laugh...? Is anything too wonderful for the Lord?... I will return to you, in due season, and Sarah shall have a son.' But Sarah denied, saying, 'I did not laugh'; for she was afraid. He said, 'Oh yes, you did laugh.'

We know, from our previous reading, that Sarah had been a beautiful young woman. We also know, from her treatment of the slave girl Hagar, that she could be spiteful. Here, we learn another flaw in the character of this great figure in the history of God's people—she was sceptical of the power of God to give her a child past childbearing age. Probably many of us would sympathize with her. It is hard to believe that something we have longed for and been denied for a long time is now to come to us, after we had given up all hope

It's a very vivid scene—the three mysterious visitors (messengers of God, angels, perhaps) with their promise that Sarah will have a son. The older woman, listening at the tent flap, not able to contain her laughter at this ridiculous idea. And the Lord, magisterial in his rebuke, especially when she denied the offence: 'Oh yes, you did laugh.'

Of course, the central point of this story isn't her unfortunate response to the promise, but God's reminder to her and her husband that nothing is too wonderful for the Lord. We may sympathize with her reaction and even feel that we might have done the same, but what she did was to question God's trustworthiness. What was now important was that she should believe the promise and, reading on, as the story unfolds, it would seem that she did.

Reflection

We may not be tempted to laugh at the promises of God, but there are plenty of other ways in which we might take them lightly.

DW

Who am I?

'So come, I will send you to Pharaoh to bring my people, the Israelites, out of Egypt.' But Moses said to God, 'Who am I that I should go to Pharaoh, and bring the Israelites out of Egypt?' He said, 'I will be with you; and this shall be the sign for you that it is I who sent you: when you have brought the people out of Egypt, you shall worship God on this mountain.' But Moses said to God, 'If I come to the Israelites and say to them, "The God of your ancestors has sent me to you", and they ask me, "What is his name?" what shall I say to them?' God said to Moses, 'I Am Who I Am.'

The story of Moses' life to this point—his birth during a time when all boy babies were being killed, his rescue from the bulrushes, his years at the royal palace and his eventual flight to the land of Midian—had simply been a preparation for this moment before the burning bush. Though he didn't know it, God had brought him thus far with a single purpose in mind, that Moses should be the leader who would take the people of Israel out of slavery and set them on the way to the Promised Land of Canaan.

It was an awesome moment and Moses was suitably overawed as God spoke to him. Yet, when the message had been spelt out, all he could do, it seems, was try to wriggle out of it. It was one objection after another: 'No one will take any notice of me!'(3:11), 'Who shall I tell them you are?' (3:13), 'Suppose they don't believe me?' (4:1), 'I'm no orator, I've never been eloquent!' (4:10) and, finally, desperately, 'Please send someone else' (4:13).

All this from the greatest leader Israel ever had, the man God spoke to 'face to face, as one speaks to a friend' (Exodus 33:11). It's a wonderful reassurance to those of us who feel that the task God's wisdom has assigned to us, whatever it may be, is beyond us. Moses felt the same, and look what he did (or rather, God achieved through him)!

Reflection

It may well be that the best possible qualifications for Christian service are that we don't feel worthy and we don't feel adequate for the task.

DW

1 KINGS 19:9–11 (NRSV)

'I am the only one'

At that place he came to a cave, and spent the night there. Then the word of the Lord came to him, saying, 'What are you doing here, Elijah?' He answered, 'I have been very zealous for the Lord, the God of hosts; for the Israelites have forsaken your covenant, thrown down your altars, and killed your prophets with the sword. I alone am left, and they are seeking my life, to take it away.' He said, 'Go out and stand on the mountain before the Lord, for the Lord is about to pass by.'

Here is yet another great servant of God in a terrible state! No one could fault Elijah's commitment, faith or courage, but, suddenly, in the face of horrible and relentless opposition, it all seems to have crumbled. It seemed nobody was on his side—God's side. All Israel had forsaken the covenant, desecrated the altars and killed God's prophets. In fact, most of that had been done by the weak king and his strong queen and the people had been too scared to oppose them. Not only that but, as Elijah was to learn, there were actually quite a lot of people like him, who had not 'bowed the knee to Baal'. So he had got the facts wrong, but when you're down it's hard to be reasonable, cool and rational.

That's why we discover the great prophet of God hiding in a cave. The voice of God puts a searching but simple question to him: 'What are you doing here, Elijah?' (that is, in hiding, v. 9).

The weary prophet's answer is to sing his song of woe again: 'There's only me left and they're after me, too'. We don't have to be great prophets or even serving God in exposed roles to know this feeling. It amounts to, 'Where's God when you need him most?'

The answer is, not hiding in a cave! Elijah was told to stand outside, in the open on the mountain and God would come to him. He wouldn't come in thunder, earthquake or wind, but in a tiny inner voice, both putting the record straight and giving him instructions for the cleansing and eventual reformation of Israel.

Reflection

Things are never so desperate that they are beyond the power and salvation of God. Honestly!

DW

2 KINGS 5:11–13 (NRSV, ABRIDGED)

Simply offensive

But Naaman became angry and went away, saying, 'I thought that for me he would surely come out, and stand and call on the name of the Lord his God, and would wave his hand over the spot, and cure the leprosy! Are not… the rivers of Damascus, better than all the waters of Israel? Could I not wash in them, and be clean?' He turned and went away in a rage. But his servants approached and said to him, 'Father, if the prophet had commanded you to do something difficult, would you not have done it? How much more, when all he said to you was, "Wash, and be clean"?'

This is part of the story of the healing of Naaman, the commander of the Aramite army (it's worth reading in full—see 1 Kings 5:1–27). The Bible calls this Gentile general a 'great man', a 'mighty warrior' and the one by whom 'the Lord had given victory to Aram', but, it adds, 'he suffered from leprosy' (5:1). Through the simple witness of a young Israelite slave in his household and the good offices of the King of Aram, he eventually presented himself at the door of the prophet Elisha in Samaria. He expected appropriate courtesies and that this noted miracle-worker would address his case personally, but, in fact, Elisha just sent a messenger to tell him to go and wash in the River Jordan seven times and then he would be cleansed of the leprosy. Hence, Naaman's indignation. Was this the way to treat a general? Not only that, but don't miracles require spectacular actions and special words? He'd brought vast sums of silver, gold and ornaments with him as payment, but the man of God seemed uninterested in them. 'Just wash!'

Naaman's reaction is one common among people who are told that eternal life through Christ Jesus is 'the free gift of God' (Romans 6:23). It can't be that easy—give me something to do. Ah, but losing status, humbly coming to 'wash', trusting God, that is 'something to do' and it can be very difficult.

Reflection

The late Donald Coggan once said that we bring nothing to our redemption except the sin from which we wish to be redeemed. Naaman could bring nothing to his healing except his leprous body and simple trust.

DW

MARK 9:21–24 (NRSV)

The cry for faith

Jesus asked the father, 'How long has this been happening to him?' And he said, 'From childhood. It has often cast him into the fire and into the water, to destroy him; but if you are able to do anything, have pity on us and help us.' Jesus said to him, 'If you are able!— All things can be done for the one who believes.' Immediately the father of the child cried out, 'I believe; help my unbelief!'

Straight after the wonderful experience of faith confirmed on the Mount of Transfiguration, the disciples had their faith challenged by the father of an epileptic boy. He had brought his son to them, but they couldn't heal him. In desperation, as Jesus came down from the mountain, he was told to bring the boy to the Lord. He told Jesus his story, how his son had had this condition since childhood, sometimes falling into the fire or into water during a fit. 'If you are able to do anything,' he pleaded, '…help us.'

Jesus' reply was enigmatic. No, he seemed to say, not if I can but if you can! It was all a question of belief—'All things can be done for the one who believes.' The father's reply is almost heart-rending in its honesty and desperation. I like the *New English Bible*'s rendering of this part: 'Lord, I have faith. Help me where faith falls short.' It isn't as literal as that above, but it captures the sense beautifully. Like most of us, he struggled to believe

and knew that he needed help.

He had grasped an important truth. Faith itself is the gift of God. We can't force ourselves to believe or screw up our determination and make ourselves do it. Faith (in the biblical sense) is trust in God and trust comes from knowing someone and remembering what they have done for us in the past. At any rate, this anguished cry for faith was answered, because Jesus healed his son, first through a command and then by lifting him to his feet and restoring him to his father.

Reflection

Honesty, like this father's, is not necessarily a substitute for faith, but it may well be the means to achieving it. If we find faith difficult, then let's pray the father's simple prayer: 'Help my unbelief'.

DW

Sunday 29 June

JOHN 11:21–27 (NRSV)

'If only'

Martha said to Jesus, 'Lord, if you had been here, my brother would not have died. But even now I know that God will give you whatever you ask of him.' Jesus said to her, 'Your brother will rise again.' Martha said to him, 'I know that he will rise again in the resurrection on the last day.' Jesus said to her, 'I am the resurrection and the life. Those who believe in me, even though they die, will live, and everyone who lives and believes in me will never die. Do you believe this?' She said to him, 'Yes, Lord, I believe that you are the Messiah, the Son of God, the one coming into the world.'

Martha was not really a doubter, but when it came to something as shocking as her brother's death, she found that her faith was severely tested. Look at her greeting to Jesus: 'If only you'd been here, he wouldn't have died.' There is not only disappointment but, surely, a touch of blame. Jesus was very dear to this family at Bethany, so why hadn't he come sooner? Bereaved people are full of such thoughts, what I call 'if only' ones.

Jesus' first attempt at comfort seems to miss the mark—'Your brother will rise again.' They were devout Jews who rejected the Sadducees' belief that there was no resurrection. She believed that her brother would rise again 'on the last day'. At that moment it wasn't the 'last day' that concerned her, but this one, so she replies, 'Oh, I know that.' Jesus turns her response into something else. He

is 'the resurrection', the source of life. Can she believe that?

Do you notice that she chooses to answer a different question? 'Yes, Lord,' she says, 'I believe you…' This is the true answer to doubt of every kind—belief not in systems and formulae, but trust in God and Jesus. What she believes about him suddenly changes what she believes about her brother. He, and she and her sister, are in the hands of someone utterly trustworthy: that is what made the difference.

Sunday reflection

When we say in church today that we believe in 'the resurrection of the body', we should ask ourselves if we really believe it.

DW

'Show me!'

Philip said to him, 'Lord, show us the Father, and we will be satisfied.' Jesus said to him, 'Have I been with you all this time, Philip, and you still do not know me? Whoever has seen me has seen the Father. How can you say, "Show us the Father"? Do you not believe that I am in the Father and the Father is in me? The words that I say to you I do not speak on my own; but the Father who dwells in me does his works. Believe me that I am in the Father and the Father is in me; but if you do not, then believe me because of the works themselves.'

Philip seems to have been one of those people who is born to ask the awkward question—mainly in his case because he wanted to know the answer! At the feeding of the 5000, it was he who pointed out the impossibly large amount of bread they would need to feed all these people in such an isolated place. Now, here, on the most solemn evening of their whole time with Jesus, he comes up with a down-to-earth suggestion to counter their problems with the things Jesus had been saying to them—'Show us the Father, and we'll be satisfied.' You bet they would! This had been the plea of people down the ages: 'show us yourself'. Moses sought permission to see God, but it was refused—'No one can see me and live.' There were visions, it's true, and signs, but being able to actually see the invisible, infinite God must await another time and another dimension of life.

Instead, Jesus invites him, and the others, to look at him, because 'The one who has seen me has seen the Father.' What a claim! If you want to know what the invisible God is like, Philip, then look at this 30-something man at the table near you. If that stretches your faith too far, then think of the things that you have seen this man do—restore sight, heal the lame, make the deaf hear, cleanse the lepers. Then tell yourself, this is what God the Father is like. This is the character and these are the works of your creator. Now believe!

Reflection

Sometimes the clue to believing is to start looking.

DW

'We had hoped'

'We had hoped that he [Jesus of Nazareth] was the one to redeem Israel... it is now the third day since these things took place. Moreover, some women of our group astounded us. They were at the tomb early this morning, and when they did not find his body there, they came back and told us that they had indeed seen a vision of angels who said that he was alive. Some of those who were with us went to the tomb and found it just as the women had said; but they did not see him.' Then he [Jesus] said to them, 'Oh, how foolish you are, and how slow of heart to believe all that the prophets have declared!'

This lovely story is of a couple—I can only assume they were Mr and Mrs Cleopas—who encountered the risen Jesus on the road to Emmaus. They had been disciples, but all their great hopes are expressed to this 'stranger' in the past tense—'we had hoped'. Now, dejected and disappointed, they are on their way home, the dream over—or so they thought. Just as the risen Jesus appeared to Mary Magdalene in her sorrow, Thomas in his scepticism and Peter in his guilt, so he drew near to this couple in their moment of dashed hope.

Jesus countered this manifestation of misery and doubt in two ways. First, he 'interpreted to them' the scriptures, giving them, on their two-hour walk, the Bible study of all Bible studies. Then, when he had joined them for a simple meal in their home, he broke the bread for them, reminding them of what had happened on Passover eve in the upper room. 'Their eyes were opened, and they recognized him' (v. 31) and, as they did, he vanished, leaving them—tiredness and despair forgotten—to hurry back the seven miles to Jerusalem to tell the others.

Christians today have both the scriptures and the sacrament. I wonder if we see them sometimes as miraculous renewers of faith? Of course, if we neglect either they can't do anything for us, but then that's obvious, isn't it?

Reflection

The object of reading the Bible is to see the purposes of God. The object of sharing in Holy Communion is to see Jesus. These are the building blocks of faith.

DW

Reluctant, but obedient

The Lord said to him [Ananias], 'Get up and go to the street called Straight, and at the house of Judas look for a man of Tarsus named Saul. At this moment he is praying, and he has seen in a vision a man named Ananias come in and lay his hands on him so that he might regain his sight.' But Ananias answered, 'Lord, I have heard from many about this man, how much evil he has done to your saints in Jerusalem; and here he has authority from the chief priests to bind all who invoke your name.' But the Lord said to him, 'Go, for he is an instrument whom I have chosen to bring my name before Gentiles and kings and before the people of Israel.'

We don't know anything about Ananias beyond this dramatic event, which was a turning point in the history of the infant Church. We can assume that he was a leading member of the Church that met in Damascus, probably secretly. Ananias may also have exercised charismatic gifts, because the conclusion of his part in the story of Saul was to lay hands on him to heal his sight and to pray that God would fill him with the Holy Spirit, so clearly he was a man of considerable faith.

Yet we see him here in a dilemma many Christians will be familiar with. The Lord tells him in a vision that a man called Saul is staying nearby. He is praying and will see in a vision Ananias—no other—coming into the house to lay hands on him to restore his sight. This really stretches Ananias' faith: 'I've heard about this Saul,' he says, 'he's done terrible things to the Christians in Jerusalem and now he's travelling around the countryside "breathing threats and murder against the disciples of the Lord" [Acts 9:1].' Some (divine) mistake, surely?

There is no mistake. So, however fearfully, Ananias goes, and the world knows the consequences—the apostleship of Paul. Sometimes faith tells us to do apparently silly and irrational things, but if—and it's a big 'if'—they are truly God's will, then only good can flow from them.

Reflection

He makes the coward spirit bold,
And calms the troubled breast.

John Newton (1725–1807)
DW

Seeing and believing

A week later his disciples were again in the house, and Thomas was with them. Although the doors were shut, Jesus came and stood among them and said, 'Peace be with you.' Then he said to Thomas, 'Put your finger here and see my hands. Reach out your hand and put it in my side. Do not doubt but believe.' Thomas answered him, 'My Lord and my God!' Jesus said to him, 'Have you believed because you have seen me? Blessed are those who have not seen and yet have come to believe.'

Poor Thomas, forever labelled 'Doubting', yet still, of course, an honoured member of the apostolic band. It's St Thomas's Day today. The other disciples have already met the risen Jesus, but Thomas was absent on that occasion. When he discovers them bursting with the news, he proceeds to pour cold water on it. He knew them—gullible clutchers at straws! 'Unless I see and touch the wounds of the nails and in his side, I won't believe.' We may assume, as Thomas had been a faithful follower of Jesus, that he was as keen as the others to believe that Jesus had risen, but he simply couldn't swallow it on the flimsy evidence of the words of the disciples. For them the wish might be father to the thought, but not for someone like him.

Then it happened! The risen Lord stood before him, offering those very wounds to his touch. We are not told that he actually touched them, but we are told that he uttered words that even went beyond the faith of the other disciples at that moment: 'My Lord and my God!'

Doubt is not, of itself, a sin. Unbelief is sin and so is disobedience. What God requires is trust and love, and Thomas seems to have had those qualities. Unlike the others, he also had a sceptical streak, a trait that always made him the 'awkward' member of the group. Some Christians feel like that, especially if their fellow church members are impatient with that kind of caution. However, they, like Thomas, will get there in the end, if in their heart of hearts they really want to believe. I reckon he did.

Reflection

Forgive my endless questions, Lord, and in your mercy meet my doubts.

DW

Finding the Way

They went through the region of Phrygia and Galatia, having been forbidden by the Holy Spirit to speak the word in Asia. When they had come opposite Mysia, they attempted to go into Bithynia, but the Spirit of Jesus did not allow them; so, passing by Mysia, they went down to Troas. During the night Paul had a vision: there stood a man of Macedonia pleading with him and saying, 'Come over to Macedonia and help us.' When he had seen the vision, we immediately tried to cross over to Macedonia, being convinced that God had called us to proclaim the good news to them.

It might be considered blasphemy to include the great apostle of faith, Paul, in a record of people in the Bible whose faith faltered under pressure. In fact, this story does not so much show him wavering or faltering as being unsure which way to turn at a particular moment in his life. For any Christians who assume that someone as open to God as he clearly was is never in that kind of doubt, the story is encouraging. For those who have yet to be in that position, it is instructive at the very least.

Paul and his companions had travelled through what we would now call central Turkey, 'having been forbidden by the Holy Spirit to preach the word in Asia'. (Yes, modern Turkey is in Asia, of course, but presumably this refers to the area further to the east and north.) We may well wonder what form this 'forbidding' took—a vision, perhaps, or strong inner prompt-ing? Perhaps all the practical arrangements broke down—the ass became lame, that kind of thing. Anyway, they didn't just sit there wondering what to do, but travelled west, towards the Aegean coast, and tried to enter Bythinia, but 'the Spirit of Jesus did not allow them'. It must have been frustrating. Didn't God want them to preach the gospel everywhere and to everybody?

Then the answer came to Paul in a night vision. A Macedonian stood there, pleading with them to 'Come over [across the Aegean]… and help us.' That convinced them and they swiftly made their way to mainland Greece. The days of hesitating, perhaps even doubting the reality of the Spirit's guidance, were over.

Reflection

Faith sometimes involves waiting!

DW

ACTS 8:30–35 (NRSV, ABRIDGED)

How can I understand?

So Philip ran up to [the chariot] and heard [the Ethiopian eunuch] reading the prophet Isaiah. He asked, 'Do you understand what you are reading?' He replied, 'How can I, unless someone guides me?' And he invited Philip to get in and sit beside him. Now the passage of the scripture that he was reading was this: 'Like a sheep he was led to the slaughter, and like a lamb silent before its shearer, so he does not open his mouth...' The eunuch asked Philip, 'About whom... does the prophet say this...?' Then Philip began to speak, and starting with this scripture, he proclaimed to him the good news about Jesus.

The eunuch—an officer of the royal court of Ethiopia—had probably travelled over 150 miles on his pilgrimage to Jerusalem. Another 120 or so miles lay ahead, possibly many more. We can assume that his journey was motivated by a religious search of some kind, but all he had so far was a copy of the book of Isaiah. A combination of the Holy Spirit and the obedient evangelist Philip made sure that it was more than enough.

We can imagine him sitting in his chariot, trying to make sense of what he was reading. Here was a man who was serious about his search for God, but listen to his heart-rending reply to the question, 'Do you understand what you are reading?': 'How can I, unless someone guides me?' That is the voice not of doubt but incomprehension. He longed to believe, but he couldn't understand. I suspect there are many people around us like that. To them, those who believe seem to speak in riddles, yet they can detect in them something that they would love to have.

Happily, the very passage the eunuch was struggling to understand was a perfect launch pad for the gospel. Jesus is the Lamb of God, 'who takes away the sin of the world'. The eunuch heard, his heart leapt, he believed and there, by the side of the road, in some desert wadi, we assume, he was baptized (v. 38).

Reflection

We should never hesitate to ask if we don't understand. We should never turn a deaf ear to those who ask us to give a reason for the faith that is in us (1 Peter 3:15).

DW

Joshua 7—12

'The Old Testament God is totally ruthless', said an agnostic celebrity in a magazine interview. 'I like that!' If we had only chapters 7—12 of Joshua to tell us about God, we might well agree. This God, who appears to support 'holy war' and 'ethnic cleansing' would be one we might worship but could hardly love.

Indeed, the book has been used in history to justify other genocides 'in the name of God'—the Crusades, the massacre of native Americans by settlers who saw America as their 'promised land' or the domination of South Africa by white colonialists. It also has disturbing resonances with the situation in Israel and Palestine today, and there is plenty of scope for Christians to misuse it in relation to that. Is there another way to approach these stories?

It should be said that we do not know whether or not the massacres happened quite as described. The book probably reached its present form many centuries after the events, though the stories preserved in it are probably more ancient. Some scholars think it was compiled to justify King Josiah's religious reforms and promote national unity. Nevertheless this still leaves us with the problem that these chapters show what Israel would have liked to do to the Canaanites!

Some solve it by just extracting the more 'spiritual' passages, such as, 'be strong and very courageous' (1:7). Some treat it as an allegory of 'spiritual warfare'. Some point out that Canaanite culture, while highly developed (they gave us the first alphabet), was bound up with a religion that involved worship that was 'violently sexual in form' (David Hinson, *History of Israel*, SPCK, 1973). It cannot have been fun being a Canaanite woman!

In grappling with this difficult book, I have discovered many ways in which it can still speak to us today. Moreover, I have gladly recognized that we do not have only this book to tell us about God. In Greek, the name 'Joshua' ('God saves'—the same as 'Hosea') is Iesous, which in Latin is Jesus. I have tried to read Joshua, as I believe we should read all the Old Testament, with Jesus always in mind.

Veronica Zundel

Self-defeated

But the Israelites broke faith in regard to the devoted things: Achan son of Carmi... took some of the devoted things; and the anger of the Lord burned against the Israelites. Joshua sent men from Jericho to Ai... and said to them, 'Go up and spy out the land.' ... Then they returned to Joshua and said to him, 'Not all the people need go up...' So about 3000 of the people went up there; and they fled before the men of Ai. The men of Ai killed about 36 of them, chasing them from outside the gate as far as Shebarim and killing them on the slope. The hearts of the people melted and turned to water.

Remember the game 'Simon says'? Anything the leader tells you to do, you do, unless they miss out the vital phrase 'Simon says'. Is God also a game-player who waits to catch us out in a misdemeanour, then withdraws his support? Three strikes and you're out? In my worst moments, I sometimes imagine God is like that.

This story might suggest just such an idea, but the reason for the defeat at Ai goes deeper. Other ancient Near East peoples fighting 'holy wars' also destroyed everything as an offering to their gods. The difference with Israel was that they saw God, not Joshua, as the true leader of the conquest. They had this confidence at Jericho. Now it has turned to complacency—'God is on our side'.

A guest preacher at my church recently said, 'God's love is both unconditional and deeply condi-tional.' The picture came to me of a university application. A university may offer an 'unconditional place', not dependent on exam results. However, once there, the student must study or be thrown out. I think it was something like that for the Israelites in Canaan. The land was promised, but they could only 'possess'—gain and keep it—on condition that they kept God's laws.

Is it the same for Christians? Yes and no. God never stops loving us, but if we do not learn to live Jesus' way, we may stop experiencing that love.

Sunday reflection

In what ways does your church help you to live for Christ daily? Take the opportunity today to thank those who help you.

VZ

Complaint to the management

Joshua said, 'Ah, Lord God! Why have you brought this people across the Jordan at all, to hand us over to the Amorites so as to destroy us? Would that we had been content to settle beyond the Jordan! O Lord, what can I say, now that Israel has turned their backs to their enemies! The Canaanites and all the inhabitants of the land will hear of it, and surround us, and cut off our name from the earth. Then what will you do for your great name?'

I read somewhere that the most common form of public prayer in the Bible is the prayer of complaint. How about your congregation—is it the most common prayer there? No, mine neither (but we're working on it!)

Joshua's frank conversation with God raises echoes of the Israelites' complaint to Moses (Exodus 16:3): 'If only we had died by the hand of the Lord in the land of Egypt, when we sat by the fleshpots'. Who did 'die by the hand of the Lord' in Egypt? The Egyptian firstborn. So, in effect, this kind of complaint is saying, 'We wish we were like the other peoples; why do we have to be different?' Joshua, likewise, seems to say, 'Why couldn't we just live where there wasn't any opposition?' As Tevye in *Fiddler on the Roof* says, 'Couldn't you just for a moment choose someone else?'

However, what interests me most here is the link Joshua makes between what happens to Israel and what people think of God. The Canaanites will 'cut off our name' and then, Joshua asks God, 'what will you do for your great name?' It is as though God's reputation is intimately bound up with the reputation of the people God has called.

We know that if we not do God's will, God will use others: 'God is able from these stones to raise up children to Abraham' (Luke 3:8). Nevertheless, what people think of the Church will often be what they think of the Church's God. All the more important, then, that we obey his command to 'bear fruits worthy of repentance' (Luke 3:8).

Reflection

Next time things go badly, express yourself frankly to God. You may be surprised at the answer!

VZ

The wages of disobedience

The Lord said to Joshua, 'Stand up! Why have you fallen upon your face? Israel has sinned; they have transgressed my covenant that I imposed on them. They have taken some of the devoted things… and they have put them among their own belongings. Therefore the Israelites are unable to stand before their enemies; they turn their backs to their enemies, because they have become a thing devoted for destruction themselves… In the morning therefore you shall come forward tribe by tribe… And the one who is taken as having the devoted things shall be burned with fire, together with all that he has, for having transgressed the covenant of the Lord, and for having done an outrageous thing in Israel.'

'If I may speak frankly…' Do you dread it when someone says that? It can be a precursor to taking us down a peg! Sometimes, though, when we take a deep breath and state our true feelings, it is the beginning of healing in a relationship.

Joshua's frank complaint had an element of 'Why can't we just be like the others?' God gives an equally robust answer: by disobeying his command, the people have indeed become like their enemies— like them in that they're headed for destruction. As dogs become like their owners (or vice versa?), we become like what we value most. Psalm 135:18 says of dumb idols, 'those who make them and all who trust them shall become like them'.

The Israelites have become like their enemies in another respect, too. Where the people of Jericho 'melt in fear' before them (2:24), now they, likewise, 'melt' before the much smaller population of Ai (7:5). The only cure is to fear God instead, for that is 'the beginning of wisdom' (Proverbs 9:10).

For Christians, though, I'm not sure that the word 'fear' is appropriate any more. Instead we love God and our neighbours, for God first loved us (1 John 4:19) Also, 'there is no fear in love… for fear has to do with punishment' (1 John 4:18). Ancient Israel, in their fear of sinning even accidentally, used the 'scapegoat' (Leviticus 16) to bear the penalty for any unknown sins among the people. There is no more punishment when another has taken the blame.

Reflection
We who follow the sin-bearer should never 'scapegoat' anyone else.

VZ

JOSHUA 7:19–25 (NRSV, ABRIDGED)

One for all

Then Joshua said to Achan, 'My son, give glory to the Lord God of Israel and make confession to him…'. And Achan answered Joshua, 'It is true; I am the one who sinned against the Lord God of Israel… when I saw among the spoil a beautiful mantle from Shinar, and 200 shekels of silver, and a bar of gold weighing 50 shekels, then I coveted them and took them…' …Then Joshua and all Israel with him took Achan son of Zerah… with his sons and daughters, with his oxen, donkeys, and sheep, and his tent and all that he had; and they brought them up to the Valley of Achor. Joshua said, 'Why did you bring trouble on us? The Lord is bringing trouble on you today.' And all Israel stoned him to death.

The other day I trapped my thumb in a wardrobe door, while standing, at my seven-year-old son's request, on an upturned washing basket (don't ask!) As I yelled in pain, I tried to reassure John that it wasn't all his fault, but he kept saying, 'Blame me, blame me, then I'll feel better.'

In troubles, we always feel better for finding someone to blame (see Jonah 1). This is how dictators justify purges and genocides. In this story, however, there really is a culprit. Achan has apparently been discovered by lot, as Jonah was (Jonah 1:7). Israel's faith is that God will provide, but Achan feels he needs to provide for himself.

His execution, with his whole family, seems harsh to us. For ancient Israel, however, sin affected a whole family (see Jeremiah 31:29–30). More than this, one person's self-centredness could threaten the whole community. Notice how our first reading said 'But Israel broke faith' (7:1). The story of Ananias and Sapphira in Acts 5 is a New Testament parallel.

The balance between community and individual is always difficult. Perhaps for any group just establishing itself, community must come first. Have we in the affluent West allowed the balance to swing too far the other way?

Reflection

'I will… make the Valley of Achor [Trouble] a door of hope' (Hosea 2:15). Use this verse from Joshua's namesake to pray for any area of trouble in the world.

VZ

The Lord gives

Then the Lord said to Joshua, 'Do not fear or be dismayed; take all the fighting men with you, and go up now to Ai... And Joshua and all Israel made a pretence of being beaten before them, and fled in the direction of the wilderness. So all the people... in the city were called together to pursue them... Then the Lord said to Joshua, 'Stretch out the sword that is in your hand towards Ai; for I will give it into your hand.'... As soon as he stretched out his hand, the troops in ambush rose quickly out of their place and rushed forward... When Joshua and all Israel saw that the ambush had taken the city and that the smoke of the city was rising, then they turned back and struck down the men of Ai.

William the Conqueror in 1066 defeated the Saxons with exactly the same technique Joshua uses here—a fake withdrawal and ambush. In Joshua's case, however, the stratagem was given directly by God.

Joshua's holding up his sword is more than a convenient signal. The sword stays up until the end of the battle, just as Moses' staff was held up while Joshua fought Amalek (Exodus 17). The conclusion of that story is Moses' statement: 'The Lord will have war with Amalek from generation to generation.' Perhaps we are meant to draw the same conclusion here, that the real conqueror is God. No part of Canaan could be conquered unless God chose to give it. In his book *Yahweh is a Warrior* (Herald Press, 1980), Millard Lind points out how the Israelites deliberately limited their military strength to demonstrate that their true leader in battle was God.

Are Christians today, however, justified in seeing any people as deserving destruction? The people of God now are not a nation, but those who follow the Prince of Peace. We must beware, therefore, identifying any modern power politics with God. A better response to Joshua would be to consider how today we could demonstrate that we too rely on God's power, not on military might.

Reflection

Emperor Constantine saw a cross in the sky and heard the words 'In this sign you will conquer'. He went on to win in battle, but did he interpret his vision rightly?

VZ

Promises to keep

Then Joshua built on Mount Ebal an altar to the Lord, the God of Israel, just as Moses the servant of the Lord had commanded... And there, in the presence of the Israelites, Joshua wrote on the stones a copy of the law of Moses, which he had written. All Israel, alien as well as citizen, with their elders and officers and their judges, stood on opposite sides of the ark in front of the levitical priests... half of them in front of Mount Gerizim and half of them in front of Mount Ebal, as Moses the servant of the Lord had commanded at the first, that they should bless the people of Israel. And afterwards he read all the words of the law, blessings and curses, according to all that is written in the book of the law.

Now and then, when I remember, I reread the Anglican wedding service, to see what I promised. I also reread insurance policies or guarantees occasionally, to see what others have promised me! The two activities are very different. One deals with legal, contractual obligations, which I could call on in court. The other is about a personal, voluntary covenant between two people to do what is best for each other in everything.

The covenant between God and Israel, symbolized here by the ark, is of the 'marriage vows' kind. People have recognized for millennia that a public commitment helps people survive in a relationship. Similarly, commitment to God's way was to help Joshua's people live in the Promised Land.

However, there are differences, too. The covenant with Yahweh is not a covenant of equals, so it rightly involves worship, an act expressing reverence and obedience. From the beginning, Israel's leadership was concerned to link living in the land with faithfulness to God's commandments.

In marriage, even when one partner breaks the vows, the other may still want to express faithfulness. Similarly, God's faithfulness was able to survive repeated betrayals by his people. There's hope for us all, then!

Reflection

'Woman, believe me, the hour is coming when you will worship the Father neither on this mountain nor in Jerusalem... But the hour is coming, and is now here, when the true worshippers will worship the Father in spirit and truth' (John 4:21–23).

VZ

83

False friends

Now... all the kings... gathered together with one accord to fight Joshua and Israel. But when the inhabitants of Gibeon heard what Joshua had done to Jericho and to Ai, they... went and prepared provisions, and took worn-out sacks for their donkeys, and wine-skins, worn-out and torn and mended, with worn-out, patched sandals on their feet, and worn-out clothes; and all their provisions were dry and mouldy. They went to Joshua in the camp at Gilgal, and said to him and to the Israelites, 'We have come from a far country; so now make a treaty with us.' ... So the leaders partook of their provisions, and did not ask direction from the Lord. And Joshua made peace with them... and the leaders of the congregation swore an oath to them.

Like Rahab in the story of Jericho, the people of Gibeon decide that discretion is the better part of valour. There is a contrast, however, with her apparently genuine belief that God was in the Israelites' invasion: 'I know that the Lord has given you the land' (2:9). The Gibeonites' 'Your servants have come from a very far country, because of the name of the Lord your God' rings less true. If the first part of the statement is a lie, how can we believe the second?

The Israelites, meanwhile, leave God entirely out of their calculations. Perhaps they are rather tired of fighting and feel an alliance dropped into their laps is not to be sneezed at, wherever it comes from. It's a fine line between 'whoever is not against us is for us' (Mark 9:40) and 'whoever is not with me is against me' (Matthew 12:30).

This story alerts us to two extremes. One is to 'take the name of the Lord in vain', which I think refers less to swearing than to tacking the name of God on to your activities in order to fend off all criticism. This is what the Gibeonites did. The other is to act without any real reference to God, whether you justify your actions by reference to common sense, saying 'that's the way the world is', or whatever. This is what Israel did. Which extreme is your usual temptation?

Prayer

'Unless the Lord builds the house, those who build it labour in vain' (Psalm 127:1). Lord, we bring our plans to you.

VZ

JOSHUA 9:22–27 (NRSV, ABRIDGED)

Count me in

Joshua summoned them, and said to them, 'Why did you deceive us, saying, "We are very far from you", while in fact you are living among us?'... They answered Joshua, 'Because it was told to your servants for a certainty that the Lord your God had commanded his servant Moses... to destroy all the inhabitants of the land before you; so we were in great fear for our lives because of you, and did this thing. And now we are in your hand: do as it seems good and right in your sight to do to us.' This is what he did for them: he saved them from the Israelites; and they did not kill them. But on that day Joshua made them hewers of wood and drawers of water for the congregation and for the altar of the Lord, to continue to this day, in the place that he should choose.

'Are they Christian?' asked an old friend when she heard that my husband and I had joined the Mennonite Church. Every human group likes to have boundaries, to know who is in and who is out, to check new members for 'soundness'.

The Gibeonites were followers of Canaanite religion, with which the Israelites were to have no compromise. Yet, because of their cunning plan, based on fear of God, not love, they find themselves permanently under contract to serve the practical needs of Israelite worship. Are they in or out? Perhaps God does not always draw the boundaries in the same places we do. In the book of Joshua, we see a Jericho prostitute saved (ch. 6) but a faithless Israelite destroyed (ch. 7). Inclusion or exclusion seems to have more to do with if you go God's way than if you name God's name.

Is it different in the New Testament, where we are 'justified by faith' (Romans 3:28)? Paul himself says no. Believers are included in the faith community by God's grace, but also for a purpose: 'For we are what he has made us, created in Christ Jesus for good works, which God prepared beforehand to be our way of life' (Ephesians 2:10). We believe, then we follow, but for some it may well be the other way round.

Prayer

Inclusive God, may our churches be places where the unsure, the seeking, the fearful are all welcomed.

VZ

JOSHUA 10:1–4, 6 (NRSV, ABRIDGED)

Friends in high places?

When King Adoni-zedek of Jerusalem heard how Joshua had taken Ai, and had utterly destroyed it... and how the inhabitants of Gibeon had made peace with Israel and were among them, he became greatly frightened, because Gibeon was a large city... and all its men were warriors. So King Adoni-zedek of Jerusalem sent a message to King Hoham of Hebron, to King Piram of Jarmuth, to King Japhia of Lachish, and to King Debir of Eglon, saying, 'Come up and help me, and let us attack Gibeon; for it has made peace with Joshua and with the Israelites.' ... And the Gibeonites sent to Joshua at the camp in Gilgal, saying, 'Do not abandon your servants; come up to us quickly, and save us, and help us....'

A couple of years ago I prayed for more friends. After my cancer diagnosis I found out how many friends I already had!

They say it's not what you know, it's who you know. Slavery in ancient Israel conferred obligations on the owner, too, so the Gibeonites here are able to turn to Israel for help.

Israel itself, however, must not depend on alliances with powerful neighbours: 'Alas for those who go down to Egypt for help... who trust in chariots because they are many and in horsemen because they are very strong, but do not look to the Holy One of Israel or consult the Lord!' (Isaiah 31:1). On the contrary, in the 'coming kingdom', all other peoples will look to God's people for guidance: 'Thus says the Lord of hosts: In those days ten men from nations of every language shall take hold of a Jew, grasping his garment and saying, "Let us go with you, for we have heard that God is with you"' (Zechariah 8:23).

Are we Christians renowned for our better way of life? A week ago as I write, 12,000 people, many Christian, met outside Parliament to lobby for justice in world trade. MPs received their information with gratitude. Meanwhile, Mennonite and Quaker churches are becoming experts in conflict mediation. If we are 'professional peacemakers', the world may beat a path to our door.

Reflection

Is your church friends with your local MP or a campaigning group? If not, why not? Pray today for Christians with political influence.

VZ

JOSHUA 10:8–13 (NRSV, ABRIDGED)

Something new under the sun

The Lord said to Joshua, 'Do not fear them, for I have handed them over to you; not one of them shall stand before you.' So Joshua came upon them suddenly, having marched up all night from Gilgal. And the Lord threw them into a panic before Israel, who inflicted a great slaughter on them at Gibeon... As they fled before Israel... the Lord threw down huge stones from heaven on them as far as Azekah, and they died; there were more who died because of the hailstones than the Israelites killed with the sword. On the day when the Lord gave the Amorites over to the Israelites, Joshua spoke to the Lord; and he said in the sight of Israel, 'Sun, stand still at Gibeon, and Moon, in the valley of Aijalon.' And the sun stood still, and the moon stopped, until the nation took vengeance on their enemies.

Have you ever prayed for something really crazy? I don't mean, 'Lord, move this paper-clip by my faith', but something that you deeply wanted that seemed impossible.

Joshua's 'crazy' prayer is for something to help him in his defeat of the army of the Amorites. From the positions of sun and moon described, he may have been asking for an extension of night, rather than day; which would also explain the Amorites' panic.

Is this an historical event or a poetic image of God's involvement in the battle? For God, nothing is impossible (Matthew 19:26) and Jesus promised that even a mustard seed-sized faith would move mountains (Matthew 17:20). However, whether history or myth, the point is the same: the battle against these five southern warlords is God's, not Israel's. Notice how the writer stresses that more died from the 'natural (or supernatural?) disaster' than by the swords of Israel.

I hope that we do not wish for our prayers to be answered by slaughter of our enemies—for we are commanded to love them (Matthew 5:44). Nevertheless, we all have impossibilities in our lives. Our battle is not against human beings, but 'spiritual forces of evil in the heavenly places' (Ephesians 6:12). This story's picture of 'something happening in the heavens' can encourage us to use spiritual, not physical, weapons.

Prayer

Bring your biggest impossibility to God today.

VZ

Those who live by the sword

Meanwhile... it was told Joshua, 'The five kings have been found, hidden in the cave at Makkedah.' Joshua said, 'Roll large stones against the mouth of the cave, and set men by it to guard them.' Then Joshua said, 'Open the mouth of the cave, and bring those five kings out to me from the cave.'... Joshua summoned all the Israelites, and said to the chiefs of the warriors who had gone with him, 'Come near, put your feet on the necks of these kings.'... And Joshua said to them, 'Do not be afraid or dismayed; be strong and courageous; for thus the Lord will do to all the enemies against whom you fight.' Afterwards Joshua struck them down and put them to death, and he hung them on five trees.

In the film *No Man's Land*, about the Bosnian war, two opposing soldiers are trapped in an abandoned trench, while a third, who had been thought dead, is lying on a bouncing mine that will kill all three if he moves. The film ends with a retreating shot of the one man left alone, lying there, after the two others have shot each other. He seemed to me to be a metaphor for the land torn apart by war.

The 'kings' in Joshua were probably no more than local warlords—a term that ten years ago might have had an antiquated ring, but which now sounds topical. We can imagine how terrified the five warlords would be, trapped in the blackness of the cave. They, in turn, had terrified others before Joshua terrified them, and so the cycle goes on.

Perhaps the symbolic action of feet on necks, however, stands for more than just the defeat of five small warlords by a stronger one. Perhaps we can take it as a sign of what God plans to do with the whole system of terror and military subjugation: to trample it under his feet. Even under the old covenant, there is a glimpse of the final peace: 'He makes wars cease to the end of the earth; he breaks the bow, and shatters the spear; he burns the shields with fire' (Psalm 46:9).

Reflection

*'Stop fighting,
and know that I am God.'*

Song by Andrew Kreider, based on
Psalm 46:10

VZ

Spiritual weapons

When King Jabin of Hazor heard of this, he sent to King Jobab of Madon, to the king of Shimron, to the king of Achshaph, and to the kings who were in the northern hill country, and in the Arabah south of Chinneroth, and in the lowland, and in Naphoth-dor on the west, to the Canaanites in the east and the west, the Amorites, the Hittites, the Perizzites, and the Jebusites in the hill country, and the Hivites under Hermon in the land of Mizpah. They came out, with all their troops, a great army, in number like the sand on the seashore, with very many horses and chariots.... And the Lord said to Joshua, 'Do not be afraid of them, for tomorrow at this time I will hand over all of them, slain, to Israel; you shall hamstring their horses, and burn their chariots with fire.'

If you have been on pilgrimage to Israel, you have probably seen the excavations at Hazor. It was a large, fortified city with room to keep many horses and chariots as well as perhaps 40,000 people within its walls—a political and military base combined. Under its king, another alliance is formed against the Israelites, this time of northern 'kings'.

What would an ordinary military commander do on capturing a city full of the latest weaponry and military transport (for 'horses and chariots' read 'tanks and warheads')? Most likely he'd readily accept this free gift to the defence budget. Israel under God's command, however, is ordered to destroy everything—chariots and the horses that power them. Horses were a military animal, but

the preferred mount for the Prince of Peace is a donkey (Matthew 21:5).

As scholars have pointed out, the only one with a chariot in ancient Israel is God: 'you make the clouds your chariot, you ride on the wings of the wind' (Psalm 104:3). Once again we learn that 'Joshua took all these kings and their land at one time, because the Lord God of Israel fought for Israel' (10:42). Not 'fought with' but 'fought for'—the victories are seen as entirely God's doing.

Prayer
Lord, help us to see what you are doing in today's conflicts and issues and to join in with your spiritual weapons.

VZ

Land rights

Joshua made war a long time with all those kings... For it was the Lord's doing to harden their hearts so that they would come against Israel in battle, in order that they might be utterly destroyed, and might receive no mercy, but be exterminated, just as the Lord had commanded Moses. At that time Joshua came and wiped out the Anakim from the hill country, from Hebron, from Debir, from Anab, and from all the hill country of Judah, and from all the hill country of Israel; Joshua utterly destroyed them with their towns... So Joshua took the whole land, according to all that the Lord had spoken to Moses; and Joshua gave it for an inheritance to Israel according to their tribal allotments. And the land had rest from war.

If the Anakim sound like something from *Star Wars*, it may not be a coincidence! Writers like to borrow exotic-sounding names with mythical assocations. The Anakim were the people seen by the spies Moses sent into the land, who returned saying, 'All the people that we saw in it are of great size... and to ourselves we seemed like grasshoppers' (Numbers 13:32–33). Only Caleb and Joshua retained their courage: 'If the Lord is pleased with us, he will bring us into this land and give it to us...' (Numbers 14:8).

It is not easy for city-dwellers like myself to really know what land meant for the people of Israel. Buying our food from supermarkets, we forget our dependence on the land and what it can produce. Yet, without access to land to grow crops and raise animals, we would all starve.

For the refugee Israelites, God's promised gift of 'a land that flows with milk and honey' (Numbers 14:8) meant the difference between life and death. The same is true for most refugees today.

What problems feel like (or perhaps really are) life and death issues to you? We no longer need to say, 'If the Lord is pleased with us' for, if we are in Christ, God says to all of us, 'This is my Son, the Beloved, with whom I am well pleased' (Matthew 3:17).

Prayer

We pray for those driven from their land, that our own and other safe lands may be welcoming to them and that all lands may have rest from war.

VZ

JOSHUA 12:7–22 (NRSV, ABRIDGED)

Ways of rejoicing

The following are the kings of the land whom Joshua and the Israelites defeated on the west side of the Jordan, from Baal-gad in the valley of Lebanon to Mount Halak, that rises towards Seir (and Joshua gave their land to the tribes of Israel as a possession according to their allotments, in the hill country, in the lowland, in the Arabah, in the slopes, in the wilderness, and in the Negeb...: the king of Jericho, one; the king of Ai, which is next to Bethel, one; the king of Jerusalem, one; the king of Hebron, one; the king of Jarmuth, one; the king of Lachish, one...; the king of Goiim in Galilee, one; the king of Tirzah, one—31 kings in all.

As I write, we've just had the World Cup and everywhere I saw England flags, drove past pubs full of people spilling out on to the pavement and heard roars of joy or groans of defeat rising.

Joshua's list of kings reads rather like the football results. Of course, it's more serious than that, with its repeated 'one' like a bell tolling the death knell of Canaanite society. Find the chapter and read the whole list aloud to experience the full chilling effect.

It's understandable to catalogue and announce victories. Notice, however, how God seems to be left out of this account. Then contrast how Paul chronicles his 'victories' in 2 Corinthians 11:24: five lots of 39 lashes, three beatings, a stoning, three shipwrecks, in danger from Gentiles, from false brothers and sisters, hungry, thirsty, cold... Rather a different kind of 'boasting'!

Compare Jesus' words just before his death: 'Jesus answered them, "The hour has come for the Son of Man to be glorified"' (John 12:23). Glorified, by experiencing execution on criminal charges? Most of us would rather have the '31 kings defeated' kind of glory than the suffering and death kind. Some churches encourage a 'success' mentality. In the kingdom of God, however, 'victory' has changed its meaning. 'The Son of God was revealed for this purpose'—not to destroy peoples, however corrupt, but 'to destroy the works of the devil' (1 John 3:8).

Meditation

'My brothers and sisters, whenever you face trials of any kind, consider it nothing but joy...' (James 1:2). Meditate on this and pray to be enabled to do it.

VZ

Jesus, Son of Man

The story of Jesus begins before time: 'In the beginning was the Word, and the Word was with God, and the Word was God... All things were made by him; and without him was not anything made that was made' (John 1:1, 3, AV). The fourth Gospel's opening words resound like a deep-toned bell. The people caught up in this story share its timeless dimensions. For, at a certain historical moment, Christ, the living Word, entered time. God the creator came into his creation and became one with apple seed, cornstalk and sheepfold, with birth and laughter, sorrow and pain. His coming transformed death into victory; total loss was changed into everlasting gain.

However, now the gospel music changes to the tolling of a single bell: he was in the world, and the world was made by him, yet the world knew him not. He came to his own and his own received him not (vv. 10–11). Have we received him or have we packaged him with our own particular religious wrapping and so fail to find him when he comes in unexpected ways? Have we parcelled him within our own needs, making it hard to hear his footsteps draw near?

Jesus stands outside the doors we guard so closely, the locked doors of our deepest fears, and we may be sure that whenever we open up and welcome him, it is he who welcomes us. The one who knocks, invites us, 'Come!'

The Jesus story isn't dull theology or moral philosophy. It isn't full of dos and don'ts. The story of the baby in the manger, the man dying in undeserved pain on a cross is something even the smallest child can understand. The Jesus story hushes noisy children and brings wonder to their eyes. It turns hardened criminals into saints. We are part of the story, too, and we are the good news the story tells!

The Jesus story is full of wonder, humour and humanity. It's been the theme of art, music, drama and poetry for two millennia. It is—as all the best stories always are—utterly simple and yet inexhaustible. Above all, the Jesus story is woven around individual people. We shall meet some of them in our readings these next two weeks and, in encountering the people who meet Jesus, we also encounter the Lord.

Jenny Robertson

The servant king

At that time Jesus came from Nazareth in Galilee and was baptized by John in the Jordan. As Jesus was coming up out of the water, he saw heaven being torn open and the Spirit descending on him like a dove. And a voice came from heaven: 'You are my Son, whom I love; with you I am well pleased.'

Jesus' baptism is recorded in all four Gospels. Luke adds a mention of the political rulers of the day with their network of intrigue and power. John the Baptist, in his rough clothes, has no political power, although people wondered if he might be the promised deliverer (Luke 3:15). John simply points to Jesus, identifying him as 'the Lamb of God, who takes away the sin of the world' (John 1:29).

There must have been a buzz of wonder as the young man from Nazareth pulled off the tunic he'd fastened into his belt to make walking easier and waded into the water. Some people may have muttered, 'Can anything good come out of Nazareth?' (John 1:46).

All four Gospels note that as Jesus, who is to take away the sins of the world, makes this public act of penitence, the Holy Spirit descends like a dove and the voice of the Father is heard. The prophecies of the old covenant and the hopes of the new are brought together in the three persons of the Trinity. The Son submits, the Spirit bears witness and the Father affirms that Jesus is his beloved Son 'in whom I am well pleased'. These words divide major religions, but behind them is the declaration of the Son's power (Psalm 2:7) and ministry (Isaiah 42:1–4).

Jesus lays aside his garments at the start of his ministry, just as he will lay them aside in the upper room and at the cross (John 13:4; 19:23). He leaves the water, wraps himself in his travel-worn clothing and walks away from the crowds with their longings and hunger. He enters the desert.

Sunday reflection

Jesus, Son of God, sin-bearer, royal king who took the form of a servant, may my worship today declare your power. May the praise of your people refresh the desert places of the world with your love.

JR

Jesus overcomes evil

And you shall remember that the Lord your God led you all the way these 40 years in the wilderness, to humble you and test you, to know what was in your heart, whether you would keep his commandments or not... Immediately the Spirit drove him into the wilderness. And he was there in the wilderness 40 days, tempted by Satan, and was with the wild beasts; and the angels ministered to him.

The desert is a bleak place. I've read that a dry wind blows by day, hot as the air from an electric dryer. At night, the temperature drops dramatically. Lions stalk their prey. The test for the people of Israel, and for Jesus, was to prove that keeping God's law mattered more than physical surroundings. The people failed (Psalm 95:10–11). Jesus did not.

At Jesus' baptism, the Holy Spirit appeared like a dove, but that same Spirit drove Jesus into the desert. Taut against the endless wind, his body dried like cloth. The sun scorched him. There was no comfort for body or soul as the elements and the evil one tested the Son of God. When we are tested, we immediately grope for armour, which usually protects us, only to find that it has rusted. In desert experiences, we discover how vulnerable we are. Stripped of protection, we learn compassion, which makes others feel accepted, not judged.

The miracles of Jesus show us that storms, sickness, even death are no constraints to the power of God. In the desert, in weakness and need, Jesus refuses to use God's power for his own ends. Matthew 4:2–11 and Luke 4:1–13 describe how the Lord defends himself against evil with the belt of truth, the breastplate of righteousness, the shoes of the gospel, the shield of faith and the sword of the Spirit, which is the word of God (Ephesians 6:13–17). God's resources are available to us, too.

Jesus won a victory and angels served him. I imagine them alighting like swans, borne on the desert wind. They spread their wings about Jesus and shelter him.

Prayer

Lord, your resources are sufficient for every desert on our pilgrim way.

JR

LUKE 8:1–3; MARK 15:40–41 (NIV, ABRIDGED)

The Lord's right-hand woman

After this, Jesus travelled about... proclaiming the good news of the kingdom of God. The Twelve were with him, and also some women...: Mary (called Magdalene) from whom seven demons had come out... and many others. These women were helping to support them out of their own means...

Some women were watching from a distance. Among them were Mary Magdalene, Mary... and Salome... Many other women... were also there.

Women followed Jesus from the start of his ministry. Home-based from earliest childhood, they must have found the raggle-taggle crowds, the constant moving about, demanding. It must have taken a lot of organization to support Jesus—the rabbi, after all, entrusted his money to the disciple who was a thief (John 12:6)—but the women stayed with Jesus to the end. They were present at the cross, watching as Jesus suffered his cruel death with no touch of kindness other than their faithful, sorrowing presence. They were at the resurrection and at the start of the young Church's story (Acts 1:14).

Women heard the good news— and the good news included them. The Jesus-community had to struggle to reject prejudice and accept one another—freedom fighters and tax collectors, men and women.

Mary Magdalene had been possessed by a demon. History and the daily headlines show how easy it is to demonize people who are different from ourselves, but whatever demons had afflicted Mary, she had been completely healed. She had a clear position of importance among the women and, after the resurrection, among the whole group of believers. Although a woman's testimony was considered invalid legally, Jesus entrusted Mary with the greatest news of all (John 20:17).

Then the woman who challenges stereotypes fades from the Christian story. Tradition later confused Mary with the woman in Luke 7, whose story we read tomorrow. St Petersburg's Hermitage Museum holds a painting by Titian, showing the Magdalene, loose hair (the sign of loose morals) streaming down her shoulders, her upturned eyes flooded with tears. I wonder how a modern artist would portray her?

Prayer

Challenge my prejudices, Lord.

JR

A woman of ill-repute

One of the Pharisees invited him to a meal. When he arrived... and took his place at table, suddenly a woman came in, who had a bad name in the town... She waited behind him at his feet, weeping, and her tears fell on his feet, and she wiped them away with her hair; then she covered his feet with kisses and anointed them with the ointment... He said... 'Your faith has saved you; go in peace.'

When a rich man gave a feast, the neighbourhood have-nots usually crowded around the open court-yard to watch the event. Some hoped for a hand-out, but perhaps some came today not because of the host, but because of his guest. Perhaps Simon invited the unconventional young rabbi to show the crowd how broad-minded and forgiving he was.

A woman pushes her way to Jesus. She stands behind him, waiting. Jesus has spent days with the poor and nights in prayer. The woman recognizes love she has never dreamt of, love willing to be wounded. Only too aware of the scandal she creates, she performs the service Simon the grudging host has denied his guest and, weeping, pours out her ointment, covering Jesus' feet with kisses, wiping them with her hair. And now Simon shows himself in his true colours. He only ever intended to promote himself and now he tries to prove Jesus wrong. Jesus responds with a story that enthrals the crowd, shames Simon and thanks the woman. She has waited, wept and served—she leaves forgiven, filled with love.

Her silent waiting is prayer, her weeping is repentance, her anointing is worship. Too often, like Simon, I fit Jesus into my schedule and approach him at my convenience while I call him 'Lord'. Like Simon, I even make a show of him. The woman shows me that worship is self-forgetful.

Jesus responds when we accept him as totally as this woman did, when we long to be moulded into his likeness. He comes to us, leaving the guests at the table, and, laying aside his long robe, he wraps the slave's towel around him and serves us.

Reflection

'Your name is as ointment poured forth... We will be glad and rejoice in you.
(Song of Solomon 1:3, 4, NKJV)

JR

New life

Jairus... fell at his [Jesus'] feet and pleaded earnestly with him, 'My little daughter is dying...' And a woman was there who had been subject to bleeding for twelve years... touched his cloak... Immediately her bleeding stopped... At once Jesus realized that power had gone out from him. He... asked, 'Who touched my clothes?' ... Then the woman... came and fell at his feet and, trembling with fear, told him the whole truth. He said to her, 'Daughter, your faith has healed you. Go in peace...' While Jesus was still speaking, some men came from the house of Jairus... 'Your daughter is dead,' they said... Jesus told the synagogue ruler, 'Don't be afraid; just believe.'

A child once complained, 'There aren't any Bible stories for little girls.' Well, there's Jairus' daughter, but the problem is the woman with her medical condition, so difficult to explain but impossible to miss out, because the sick girl dies while Jesus is busy with the needs of this outcast woman.

As I mulled this over, I read a novel by Yiddish writer Isaac Bashevis Singer. A Gentile woman learned how to keep kosher at that 'time of the month', when, it is believed, like the woman in the Gospel, she defiled everything she touched. Until then, I had thought that Mark's Gospel had been hastily written. Now I see that it is skilfully constructed. The infirm woman had been 'dead' to her family for twelve years; Jairus' daughter is twelve years old. Jesus calls the healed woman 'daughter' and the dead child is a daughter, too.

The disciples chafe at the delay. Surely Jesus doesn't really think that the outcast woman is more important than the influential Jairus? And now the synagogue leader's daughter is dead. Jairus has humbled himself in front of the crowd, given way to an unclean woman for nothing. Oh, Jesus, what are you expecting from this distraught father? 'Just believe' (v. 36). Is it so easy? Like Jairus, we pray to you. We follow you, struggling to keep close. Then things go wrong. Our greatest fears are realized, yet Jesus stands there, calmly saying, 'Don't be afraid; just believe.' Like the outcast who has become a daughter, Jairus must learn that he can bring Jesus nothing except his trembling belief.

Reflection
Don't be afraid; just believe.

JR

Friday 25 July

MARK 5:40–43 (NIV, ABRIDGED)

Not dead, but asleep

[Jesus] took the child's father and mother and the disciples who were with him, and went in where the child was. He took her by the hand and said to her, *'Talitha koum!'* (which means, 'Little girl... get up!') Immediately the girl stood up and walked around (she was twelve years old). At this they were completely astonished. He gave strict orders not to let anyone know about this, and told them to give her something to eat.

'The child is... but asleep', says Jesus (v. 39) and the hired mourners mock him. Jesus, though, speaks with the simplicity of great faith that focuses on the Father and not on the circumstances around him. It leads him to judgement and agony. The simplicity of Jesus leads him to the cross. The simplicity of Jesus awakens the motionless body of the twelve-year-old girl.

The disciples watch. Would the voice that rebuked the wind and calmed the gale call life back to the child? Will Jesus order the death he calls 'sleep' to leave the child as he had commanded countless demons to leave the naked, tormented outcast? (Mark 4:35—5:20). Will he restore the twelve-year-old girl to life as he has just restored a twelve-years 'dead' woman?

Jesus speaks tenderly—the words are recorded in his own language: *'Talitha koum.'* These are not the words of power. They are simple, family words, the words of the rabbi who teaches, 'When you pray, say, "Our Father"'. They are the words of a big brother in Nazareth who wakens his little sister curled on her sleeping mat as the first light of day comes shining over the flat roofs of the houses.

The girl, understanding the simple words, gets up. Now Jesus, who made the frightened woman admit in front of a huge crowd that she had touched him, orders the astonished parents to say nothing. A child brought back from the dead is a wonder to hit the headlines. A little sister roused from sleep is an everyday occurrence, as commonplace as bread—and surely the child needs some breakfast after that long, deep sleep.

Reflection

God delights in simplicity—bread and wine, lilies, sparrows, baked fish by the lakeside, a sleeping child (Psalm 131:2).

JR

Five small loaves make a miracle

When Jesus... saw a great crowd coming towards him, he said to Philip, 'Where shall we buy bread for these people to eat?' ... Andrew, Simon Peter's brother, spoke up, 'Here is a boy with five small barley loaves and two small fish, but how far will they go among so many?' ... Jesus then took the loaves, gave thanks and distributed to those who were seated as much as they wanted. He did the same with the fish.

All four Gospels record this miracle. In the first three, the disciples ask, 'How shall we feed this crowd?' while in John's Gospel Jesus challenges the disciples with the need and Andrew brings a boy who offers all he has. Yesterday we saw that a daughter's death is simply sleep. Today, bread and fish feed a multitude. The food could not be more normal, the feeding simpler, yet the numbers fed (v. 10) more extraordinary. God delights in simplicity, in the everyday that we often take for granted. What is one packed lunch among so many?

My daughter and I watched a video in which young adults talked about daily lives made possible because of anti-psychotic medication. We saw them shopping, caring for a child, talking to friends, cooking, 'Just ordinary things, you know' one woman said. 'Just ordinary things' are denied my daughter, 'dead' for twelve years with severe mental illness, in and out of hospital, hostels, council housing.

She has been evicted five times. She has had eight addresses in as many years, the hated hospital the only constant factor. She has been brought in by taxi, ambulance, police car, held down and forcibly injected. She has had an army of support workers, consultants, lawyers. She has lost most of her friends. She has lost the right to care for her child. I hold on, trying to derive comfort in the everyday, waiting for the miracle, believing in the loaves and fishes, believing abundance is offered. I often use the following prayer.

Prayer

Almighty God, we have no power of ourselves to help ourselves: keep us both outwardly in our bodies and inwardly in our souls: that we may be defended from all adversities which may happen to the body, and from all evil thoughts which may assault and hurt the soul.

Book of Common Prayer

JR

Mind that gap!

As Jesus started on his way, a man ran up to him and fell on his knees before him. 'Good teacher,' he asked, 'what must I do to inherit eternal life?' … Jesus looked at him and loved him. 'One thing you lack,' he said. 'Go, sell everything you have and give to the poor, and you will have treasure in heaven. Then come, follow me.' At this the man's face fell. He went away sad, because he had great wealth.

Mark's Gospel is carefully constructed. After the desert, events take place in Capernaum, by the lakeside and along the road leading to Jerusalem where the final drama is played out. Here is a roadside scene. A young ruler (Matthew 19:16–22; Luke 18:18–23) encounters Jesus and discovers the gap in his life.

We may imagine that he loved life, loved the hard, hot road over which his sandalled feet ran, loved good times with his friends, laughter and red wine, keeping festivals and fasts, quiet times of prayer, intoning ancient psalms. However, he knew he couldn't hold on to these things when death came. That gap led him to Jesus and he asks, 'Good teacher, what must I do to inherit eternal life?' He awaits the reply eagerly. Yes, keep the commandments—all the teachers said that, although there were rumours that this rabbi interpreted the law differently and often flagrantly flouted it.

Looking at his questioner, aglow with life and longing for life, Jesus loved him. He saw the real gap in his life and challenged him with the one thing that this young man who had everything lacked: 'Give your goods to the poor and follow me.' The happy story has a sad ending: the young man goes away sorrowfully.

Some 1100 years later, a well-to-do young man in Assisi obeyed these words and devoted his life to the poor for the love of Christ. His influence still refocuses lives and challenges lifestyles. In our own time, an old woman in Calcutta took Christ into her arms every time she nursed a dying beggar. I have seen Mother Theresa's young nuns in blue-edged white saris ankle-deep in slush in St Petersburg and Warsaw. The thing that seems too hard turns out to be the true answer—with eternal treasure at the end.

Prayer
Lord, fill my gaps with praise today.

JR

JOHN 8:1–9 (NIV, ABRIDGED)

Prayer in the night

But Jesus went to the Mount of Olives. At dawn he appeared again in the temple courts.... [They]... brought in a woman caught in adultery... and said to Jesus, 'Teacher... In the Law Moses commanded us to stone such women. Now what do you say?' They were using this question as a trap... Jesus bent down and started to write on the ground with his finger... 'If any one of you is without sin, let him be the first to throw a stone at her.' ... At this, those who heard began to go away... until only Jesus was left, with the woman still standing there.

A Gaelic proverb says, 'Night is a good herdsman, bringing all creatures home.' After the day's work is done, lamps are lit, families gather to eat. Babies are hushed to sleep. The doors are shut.

However, Jesus is outside. Perhaps he kindled a fire and lay beside it, watching sparks fly up towards the stars until sleep blotted out the night. Perhaps he sat meditating on the scriptures he loved so well. Perhaps he prayed, climbing the night like a ladder to God in a communion that sustained him more than sleep.

Danger and controversy are never far from Jesus and, early next morning, he is confronted with a guilty woman. Even as I write, a woman in a Muslim state awaits death by stoning while the world pleads for mercy. Jesus has left an example for compassionate justice to this day, but the woman whose reprieve Jesus wins stands before a teacher whom the religious leaders are intent on destroying. Her trial is his trial also. Jesus conducts himself in silence, bending towards the ground, writing in the dust. This is not the silence of indifference and it is certainly not the silence of cowardice. Jesus is as well-versed in the law as the teachers. He applies Deuteronomy 17:7 to the fraught situation, but he makes a significant change: let the one without sin throw the first stone.

The result is dramatic: the woman and he are left alone, face to face, as one day we shall be also, waiting for his word. He says to her, 'Neither do I condemn you' (v. 11).

Reflection

Bearing sin and scoffing rude,
in my place condemned he stood,
sealed my pardon with his blood...

Philip Bliss (1838–76)

JR

JOHN 11:25–27, 40, 43 (NIV, ABRIDGED)

I am the resurrection and the life

Jesus said to her [Martha], 'I am the resurrection and the life. He who believes in me will live, even though he dies; and whoever lives and believes in me will never die. Do you believe this?' 'Yes, Lord,' she told him. 'I believe that you are the Christ, the Son of God, who was to come into the world.' ... Then Jesus said, 'Did I not tell you that if you believed, you would see the glory of God? ... 'Lazarus, come out! ... Take off the grave clothes and let him go.'

We have encountered Jesus' compassion, his deep trust in God, his insight into people's innermost thoughts. Today, the Feast of Mary, Martha and Lazarus, we note the earthly friendships he enjoyed, his prayerful union with the Father he so intimately calls 'Abba' and his unparalleled power as he summons Lazarus from the grave.

On the eve of his execution, Jesus demonstrates his victory over death. He makes it plain that he plans to reveal God's glory (vv. 4, 40). We get a glimpse into the character of Thomas, who fears the outcome but doggedly goes along; 'Let us also go,' he tells the others, 'that we may die with him' (v. 16). Jesus drew this deep loyalty from the disciples even when they didn't fully understand him and that encourages us when the going's tough and we can't quite believe it will get better.

Tomorrow we'll focus in depth on Jesus' emotional response. Let's watch him approach the tomb. Martha and Mary are with him—sisters who are close friends of his. Jesus has enjoyed the welcome of their home in Bethany (Luke 10:38–42; John 12:1–9) and they have both declared their faith in him. Martha, who runs to meet Jesus, is given the main dialogue, while Mary falls at his feet with a stammered confession of faith (vv. 21–27, 32). Mourning friends surround the sisters. In spite of Martha's frank objection, the heavy stone is pushed away as Jesus prays, 'Abba, Father...'. The prayer shows how truly 'I and the Father are one' (John 10:30).

In obedience to the Lord's command, Lazarus emerges, bound in grave-clothes. The victory is won.

Reflection

'He who believes in me will live, even though he dies...'
Do you believe this?

JR

Tears costlier than jewels

When Mary reached the place where Jesus was and saw him, she fell at his feet and said, 'Lord, if you had been here, my brother would not have died.' When Jesus saw her weeping, and the Jews who had come along with her also weeping, he was deeply moved in spirit and troubled. 'Where have you laid him?' he asked. 'Come and see, Lord,' they replied. Jesus wept.

I went once to one of Warsaw's smallest theatres, rebuilt from the rubble of the wartime ghetto. If stones could speak, these would cry out and weep. I watched a performance of Tchaikovsky's *Eugene Onegin* —an opera beloved of my friends in St Petersburg. In the last act, Onegin sings, 'You weep? These tears are more precious than jewels'.

Approaching the tomb of his dear friend, Jesus wept. He is in danger of his life (vv. 8, 16, 49–53), but he doesn't weep for himself. Martha, Mary and their friends lament in the customary way, just as the hired mourners outside Jairus' home wailed (Mark 5:38), just as Jesus himself will grieve over Jerusalem (Luke 19:41). Jesus, witnessing their grief, is 'deeply moved' (vv. 33, 38). We can be sure that he feels that same deep anger when children are violated, when bombs tear homes apart, when thousands starve while the rich world abuses the planet.

This wonderful passage in John's Gospel reveals that while Jesus, who has come to bring everlasting life (John 3:16), expresses anger at the fact of death, he also experiences up-welling emotion and personal sorrow that he is not ashamed to show. The shortest verse in the Bible is one of the most profound. We will never plumb the depths of those tears.

El Greco, one of the most intense and mysterious Christian artists, depicts Christ embracing the cross, his upturned eyes awash with unshed tears. Just such tears, said Aida of Leningrad, twice on trial for her faith, welled deep in the eyes of long-suffering Russian women whose children had been ridiculed, abused and removed from home because of the parents' Christian beliefs. I think Jesus wept then, too. When his friends sorrow, Jesus weeps—and are we not his friends, too?

Reflection

A man of sorrows and acquainted with grief.

JR

The tree to the top

Zacchaeus... wanted to see who Jesus was... So he ran ahead and climbed a sycamore-fig tree... When Jesus reached the spot, he looked up and said... 'Zacchaeus, come down immediately. I must stay at your house today.' So he came down at once and welcomed him gladly... Zaccheus stood up and said to the Lord, 'Look Lord! Here and now I give half of my possessions to the poor, and if I have cheated anybody out of anything, I will pay back four times the amount.' Jesus said... 'Today salvation has come to this house, because this man, too, is a son of Abraham. For the Son of Man came to seek and to save what was lost.'

The tax collector had only climbed one tree in his life: the tree to the top. The malpractices that feathered his own nest beggared one family after another and closed the doors of the synagogue against him, but Zacchaeus had hardened his heart so often that his capacity for love had shrivelled. Self-interest blocks our emotions and Zacchaeus' soul shrank as his wealth increased. That is, until Jesus came to town.

Zacchaeus had no false illusions—he knew no one would make way for him. A true entrepreneur, he immediately ran ahead and found a grandstand view in a handy tree. Jesus stopped and looked up, recognition and welcome shining in his whole countenance, as though the sun had come out from a cloud. Zacchaeus held his breath—could such welcome be for him? Anger, resentment, scorn were what he usually saw, but Jesus had seen the hunger in the rich man's heart. His challenge was imperative and immediate and Zacchaeus' response was prompt and radical. Now, on the way to his Passion, Jesus returned a lost son to the fold of Israel. By being ready to bend the law to the point where he seemed to break it (in this case by entering the tax-collector's house), Jesus brought salvation to this sinful dealer. The amazed crowd eagerly snatched at the rich man's freely offered goods. Zaccheus stands in his emptied house with a full heart and Jesus goes on his way to be condemned by the same law to which he has restored the tax-collector.

Prayer

Lord, come and stay
in my house today.

JR

Simon of Cyrene carries the cross

A certain man from Cyrene, Simon, the father of Alexander and Rufus, was passing by on his way in from the country, and they forced him to carry the cross. They brought Jesus to the place called Golgotha (which means The Place of the Skull). Then they offered him wine mixed with myrrh, but he did not take it. And they crucified him.

Jesus is on the road to death. Tradition says that he fell under the cross, but the Gospels do not record this. Simon, who had perhaps made a long journey to Jerusalem for Passover, is forced to carry the cross. Now his Passover is ruined, for although it was an act of mercy to weep for a condemned man, Simon has been made unclean by his contact with the cross. However, pressed into shameful, public forced labour, Simon may have become a follower of Jesus. Luke says that Simon walked behind Jesus, the mark of a disciple (Luke 23:26). If so, Simon's life changed because of that moment of shame as he was to carry the cross of Jesus in his heart from then on.

We don't know if he stayed to watch Jesus die or if he shrank back into the crowd. Perhaps he sought out the disciples, anxious to learn more. Simon and his sons were well-known in the early Church—why else would Mark mention them? Paul greets 'Rufus, chosen in the Lord' (Romans 16:13). I like to think that Simon was one of the Cyreneans who worked with the church in Antioch (Acts 13:1).

Perhaps to the end of his days, Simon sorrowed that he had not stepped forward of his own free will to help Jesus. Similarly, a teacher in Nazi Germany, a decent man, heart-sick at daily cruelties, saw a Jewish pupil mistreated by police. Not wanting to shame the boy, he looked away. I would have looked away as well.

Yet, unwillingly serving the most broken of men, Simon found that the Messiah had visited him that Passover day not in triumph, but in need and shame. This is the meaning of the gospel Jesus taught in word and deed until he spelt it out in his own body, wretchedly spread on a cross for all to see.

Prayer
Lord, teach me not to look away.

JR

Follow me

When they [the disciples] landed, they saw a fire of burning coals there with fish on it, and some bread... Jesus said to them, 'Come and have breakfast.' ... When they had finished eating, Jesus said to Simon Peter, 'Simon, son of John, do you truly love me more than these?' 'Yes, Lord,' he said, 'you know that I love you.' Jesus said, 'Feed my lambs... Take care of my sheep.'

In this chapter, one of the most mysterious and moving in John's Gospel, Jesus ministers to his disappointed disciples, challenges and commissions Peter and, in the process, speaks profoundly and intimately to us all.

It's dawn at the lakeside. The disciples had returned to their old trade—and caught nothing. Jesus appears on the shore, but they don't recognize him (vv. 1–4). He gives them a sign—a net so heavy that they can hardly drag it ashore (v. 6). The men who have been working all night see a fire at the lakeside and wonder who could have made it? They catch the appetizing aroma of sizzling fish—who could have cooked it? The Lord himself has provided breakfast for his friends.

Sometimes, when we are disappointed and spiritually hungry, we feel our lives are as empty as the disciples' net, but then dawn streaks the sky and, oh, wonder! Christ walks by the shore and calls us. It could be in a letter or e-mail from a friend. It could be literally a sunrise sweeping over the dark horizon. He feeds us afresh with his word, comforts us with his presence. Then he challenges us: 'Do you love me?' Broken-hearted like Peter, we reply, 'Lord, you know that I love you.' Then he challenges us yet again, 'Feed my lambs. Take care of my sheep... Follow me.'

Follow me! Yes, even when you are so spiritually disabled that someone else must 'dress you and lead you' (v. 18) by praying for you, upholding you and giving you new direction. Yes, even when you are so frail that others must literally care for you, you are still a disciple. You must follow Jesus still and the light at the lakeside will brighten your days, the fire the Lord lit will warm you and then the fish, the little silver fish from Lake Galilee, will feed you.

Prayer

Thank you, Lord!

JR

'Our God reigns': Some minor prophets

The prophets called people back to their spiritual roots, speaking in the name and power of God both to their contemporaries and those who would follow. Over the next two weeks we will be looking at four of the twelve 'minor prophets'—Obadiah, Micah, Nahum and Haggai. I remember from my college days that our Old Testament lecturer introduced them as 'the little-read prophets', which I heard as 'the little red prophets', conjuring up a wonderful picture of small red men, running in line behind each other into battle! Little-known, little-read, relegated to a minor league, have they any value for us today?

Obadiah is odd in that no one really knows who he was, and his book is the shortest in the Old Testament, just one chapter, but he packs a powerful punch with his prophecy. It is testimony to the God who rules the nations, who is sovereign for all time.

Micah, a younger contemporary of Isaiah, denounced the social evils of his time, and of ours, too. He sets out so clearly and without compromise God's ways of justice and peace, the blessings of obedience and the glorious promise of the Saviour who would come from Bethlehem.

Nahum was a prophet from Elkosh. We cannot say for certain when he prophesied, but his preaching concerning the city of Nineveh puts him somewhere in the 600s BC. He proclaims good news for those who will keep their vows to God, but wholesale destruction of the wicked. However powerful they may seem, they will be brought down and there will be no one to help them.

Haggai had words of rebuke for the people who had been so busy building themselves beautiful, comfortable homes that they had left God's house in ruins. He shames them into action, encourages them with a vision of what can and must be, with a reminder that 'the silver is mine, the gold is mine, says the Lord of hosts' (2:8)—words that should be written large on our hearts in our 21st-century consumer-led society. 'Keep your promises, put God first, get to work for him' was the thundering message of Haggai.

Different people, different situations, but all echoing one triumphant theme in their prophecies: 'our God reigns'. They bring challenge, judgment, assurance, and words for today to encourage us to battle on for the Lord and to victory.

Margaret Cundiff

The mighty brought low

The vision of Obadiah. Thus says the Lord God concerning Edom: We have heard a report from the Lord, and a messenger has been sent among the nations: 'Rise up! Let us rise up against it for battle!' I will surely make you least among the nations; you shall be utterly despised. Your proud heart has deceived you, you that live in the clefts of the rock, whose dwelling is in the heights. You say in your heart, 'Who will bring me down to the ground?' Though you soar aloft like the eagle, though your nest is set among the stars, from there I will bring you down, says the Lord.

Obadiah's name means 'servant of the Lord' or 'worshipper of Yahweh'. Not an uncommon name and we have record of at least a dozen in the Old Testament. Apart from the writing that bears his name, we know nothing about him, yet this one chapter has been recorded for all time including ours.

Today we read the stern words of judgment on Edom, Judah's long-time enemy. The Edomites seemed invincible and unstoppable, sweeping all before them, cruel and calculating, confident in their proven ability to overcome all nations and reign supreme. The picture is of a rock-solid power, sweeping away opposition with seemingly super-human strength from an impenetrable base, without fear of God or man. Yet Obadiah prophesies that they would be brought down, utterly destroyed and made a laughing stock by the one they had not reckoned with—the Lord God.

Did those who listened to the words of Obadiah believe the prophecy? It would seem totally impossible, at best wishful thinking, or the ranting of a religious zealot, but did it come to pass? History shows that it did. Edoms come and go, kingdoms rise and fall—the pages of history are littered with them—but the power of the Lord remains and triumphs because he alone is God. The reminder in our reading today serves both to humble and encourage us to acknowledge him supreme in our own lives and live accordingly.

Sunday reflection and prayer

'The kingdom of the world has become the kingdom of our Lord and of his Messiah, and he will reign for ever and ever' (Revelation 11:15). Lord, help me to know, obey and rejoice in your kingship in my life, today and always.

MC

Obadiah 10–14 (NRSV, abridged)

Family responsibility

For the slaughter and violence done to your brother Jacob, shame shall cover you, and you shall be cut off for ever. On the day that you stood aside, on the day that strangers carried off his wealth, and foreigners entered his gates and cast lots for Jerusalem, you too were like one of them. But you should not have gloated over your brother, on the day of his misfortune... you should not have boasted on the day of distress. You should not have... joined in the gloating over Judah's disaster on the day of his calamity; you should not have looted his goods on the day of his calamity. You should not have stood at the crossings to cut off his fugitives; you should not have handed over his survivors on the day of distress.

Edom gloated over the fall of its brother nation, Judah. Not only that, but its people took full advantage of the people of Judah's misery for their own gain as the spoils of war, siding with the enemy, making capital out of Judah's defeat, even more than the strangers and foreigners who had overrun Jerusalem. Yet Edom and Judah were in a blood relationship, related by Esau and Jacob. It was a fraught relationship from the beginning, but, nevertheless, they had a God-given responsibility to help one another and they chose to disregard it totally.

We may not consider that we are anything like those who were denounced so fiercely, but perhaps we need to re-examine our attitude towards others who may seem very distant from us, but who are used and abused because they are vic-tims of their past. What about the crippling debts of poorer countries, people held to ransom because of them and so unable to make a fresh start? Do we protest against injustice, actively engage in championing their cause, or shrug our shoulders, even indirectly benefiting from their misery?

We are part of one world, God's world, part of his family, brothers and sisters for whom Christ died. A reading of Matthew 25:31–46 concerning the final judgment may put it into perspective for us.

Prayer

Lord, may I never see another's weakness or misfortune as a means of gain, but an opportunity to share and serve in your name and for your sake.

MC

Whose world is it anyway?

Hear, you peoples, all of you; listen, O earth, and all that is in it; and let the Lord God be a witness against you, the Lord from his holy temple. For lo, the Lord is coming out of his place, and will come down and tread upon the high places of the earth. Then the mountains will melt under him and the valleys will burst open, like wax near the fire, like waters poured down a steep place. All this is for the transgression of Jacob and for the sins of the house of Israel. What is the transgression of Jacob? Is it not Samaria? And what is the high place of Judah? Is it not Jerusalem?

Micah came from Moresheth (v. 1), 25 miles south-west of Jerusalem. We know the times he lived in, but of the prophet himself we know nothing more. We are given the specific area of his prophecy, Samaria and Jerusalem, but his words have a bearing for all people of all times, including our own. He deals with social, economic and moral issues; he exposes the misuse of power, corruption, extortion, fraud and the spin doctors of the religious and state authorities. He proclaims that there is no escape from the judgment of God, no one is beyond his authority.

The picture we have here is of the effect of sin not only on people, but also on the environment. It is a graphic description of what would be called a 'natural disaster' today, but something also brought about by what has been called 'the rape of the earth'. How we use what God has given us affects not only us and ours but the people down the road, across the country, throughout the world. Our use of the earth's resources, how we dispose of our rubbish, whether we care about how our foodstuffs are produced, what we put into the rivers and seas, bury underground or release into the atmosphere—in all of this we are subject to God's judgment. We answer to him.

Reflection

'In his hand are the depths of the earth; the height of the mountains are his also. The sea is his, for he made it, and the dry land, which his hands have formed' (Psalm 95:4–5). How will my stewardship be judged?

MC

Does it really matter?

Alas for those who devise wickedness... on their beds! When the morning dawns, they perform it, because it is in their power. They covet fields and seize them; houses, and take them away; they oppress householder and house, people and their inheritance. Therefore, thus says the Lord: Now, I am devising against this family an evil from which you cannot remove your necks; and you shall not walk haughtily, for it will be an evil time.' ... 'Do not preach'—thus they preach—'one should not preach of such things; disgrace will not overtake us.' Should this be said, O house of Jacob? Is the Lord's patience exhausted? Are these his doings? Do not my words do good to one who walks uprightly?

Here is powerful condemnation of those who sin but make sure they keep within the law to further their own ends, who plot and plan to take advantage of the poor and weak, those without means to reply. Yet they still want more and more, covet what others have and devise ways to obtain it. Because of their power it is convenient that these practices are overlooked. After all, who will rock the boat, incur their displeasure? Micah does. He exposes them for what they are, spells out their sin and the consequences.

However, there are other preachers who say that God is a loving God, who cares for his people. Whatever they may have done, he forgives them, for he would not hurt his own people, they say. They rebuke Micah for daring to speak out in such a harsh way.

After all, 'business is business'. God will understand, nothing will happen. They have conveniently forgotten that God's law has been broken, the commandment 'you shall not covet' violated. We are all prone to desire what others have, but thank God for his messengers, prophets of yesterday and today who have the courage and power to challenge us as to our own lifestyles before it is too late. As Jesus reminds us, 'Take care! Be on your guard against all kinds of greed; for one's life does not consist in the abundance of possessions' (Luke 12:15).

Prayer

Lord, thank you for your faithful servants who speak your word without fear or favour. May I always hear, heed and obey.

MC

In name only

Hear this, you rulers of the house of Jacob and chiefs of the house of Israel, who abhor justice and pervert all equity, who build Zion with blood and Jerusalem with wrong! Its rulers give judgment for a bribe, its priests teach for a price, its prophets give oracles for money; yet they lean upon the Lord and say, 'Surely, the Lord is with us! No harm shall come upon us.' Therefore because of you Zion shall be ploughed as a field; Jerusalem shall become a heap of ruins, and the mountain of the house a wooded height.

What a decadent picture we have here of the leadership of the city! Those who should have been guiding the people according to God's commandments, building up the people of God as a holy nation, were rotten to the core, achieving their ends by corrupt methods and exploitation. Determined to build a powerful nation, they were completely at odds with what they claimed to stand for. At every layer of authority there was corruption, and that included the religious leaders. What an indictment—the priests would only teach if they were paid, having no sense of being God's stewards of sacred truth, with the privilege and responsibility of service. The frightening thing about all this is that they felt quite secure because they made outward observance of their religion. They acknowledged God in their religious practices, but went their own selfish and sinful way the rest of the time. They 'lean upon the Lord'—in other words, saw him as a good luck charm, an insurance policy there to protect them, regardless of what they did.

More than ever today we hear the term 'nominal' used to describe Christian countries, communities and individuals. In fact, there is almost a pride in being so described, as though it makes it all right merely to give lip-service to Jesus Christ. However, nominal—'in name only'—is false security, like the house in the story that Jesus told, built on the sand and collapsing in ruins when the storm comes. We need to examine ourselves constantly in the light of God's word, and build on Christ, our only sure foundation.

Reflection

Is my faith built on solid rock or sinking sand?

MC

Pilgrims on the way

In days to come the mountain of the Lord's house shall be established as the highest of the mountains... many nations shall come and say: 'Come, let us go up to the mountain of the Lord, to the house of the God of Jacob; that he may teach us his ways, and that we may walk in his paths.' For out of Zion shall go forth instruction, and the word of the Lord from Jerusalem. He shall judge between many peoples... they shall beat their swords into ploughshares, and their spears into pruning hooks; nation shall not lift up sword against nation, neither shall they learn war any more; but they shall all sit under their own vines and under their own fig trees, and no one shall make them afraid; for the mouth of the Lord of hosts has spoken.

There is a rhyme that goes, 'Two men looked out from prison bars; one saw mud, the other stars.' Often as we look at what is happening in the world, in the Church and even in our own lives, all we see is a quagmire, a churned-up muddy mess and we feel ourselves being sucked into it, hopeless and helpless. Yet, as we raise our heads and our hearts to God, we realize that there is hope, sure and certain, the promise of a new beginning.

In John 12:32, we have the promise of Jesus: 'And I, when I am lifted up from the earth, will draw all people to myself.' He was lifted up high on the cross when he died to save us, and he is now lifted high in heaven where he reigns in glory. One day all nations, all peoples will acknowledge him. As we keep our eyes fixed on him, we will be led in the way of the Lord. We have already begun the journey and one day it will be completed, but for now we travel on in faith together, keeping the vision ever before us. In today's reading we have a foretaste of heaven, so take time to enjoy it!

Reflection

Grow in the grace and knowledge of our Lord and Saviour Jesus Christ. To him be the glory both now and to the day of eternity. Amen.
(2 Peter 3:18)

MC

Meekness and majesty

But you, O Bethlehem of Ephrathah, who are one of the little clans of Judah, from you shall come forth for me one who is to rule in Israel, whose origin is from old... Therefore he shall give them up until the time when she who is in labour has brought forth; then the rest of his kindred shall return to the people of Israel. And he shall stand and feed his flock... in the majesty of the name of the Lord his God. And they shall live secure, for now he shall be great to the ends of the earth; and he shall be the one of peace.

This passage immediately leads me to think of Christmas, of that 'little town of Bethlehem' and the one who was born there in such humble surroundings. The promise was fulfilled and God's gift given not only to his people, but also to all who would accept Jesus as Saviour. What did it say, though, to the people of Micah's day? They would look back longingly to the shepherd king David, who had come from such lowly beginnings, and take hope from God promising to send them a new David to pastor and lead them, the Messiah to whom they were looking for rescue.

The expectations of the Messiah were compounded by generations on generations, but when he did come, he was recognized and accepted only by a few. He was seen as a danger, a threat to be disposed of, buried and forgotten, but as Peter testified on the day of Pentecost, 'This Jesus God raised up, and of that all of us are witnesses' (Acts 2:32) and 'let the entire house of Israel know with certainty that God has made him both Lord and Messiah, this Jesus whom you crucified' (Acts 2:36). Here is God's anointed one from the very beginning, now revealed and glorified. He cannot be confined to a stable in Bethlehem or to a cross at Calvary. Not all the world's armies can defeat him, nor powers of earth thwart his purposes, and to all those who acknowledge him he gives his blessing of peace.

Reflection

May the God of hope fill you with all joy and peace in believing, so that you may abound in hope by the power of the Holy Spirit.
(Romans 15:13)

MC

Micah 6:6–8 (NRSV)

What is required of me?

'With what shall I come before the Lord, and bow myself before God on high? Shall I come before him with burnt offerings, with calves a year old? Will the Lord be pleased with thousands of rams, with ten thousands of rivers of oil? Shall I give my firstborn for my transgression, the fruit of my body for the sin of my soul?' He has told you, O mortal, what is good; and what does the Lord require of you but to do justice, and to love kindness, and to walk humbly with your God?

How can I get round God? How can I impress him with my sincerity? What would prove to him how good I am, how religious and how worthy I am of his personal attention?

Ridiculous, isn't it, thinking that they could influence God like that and yet still behave as they did? Before we condemn them, why not translate it into modern terms? It is so easy to make a donation to mission and ignore the needs of a neighbour, spend hours working for the Church and turn a blind eye to a community project, even preach the most eloquent sermons but never open our mouths on behalf of human rights. Do we ever question our own motives? We know what God requires of us—it is clearly expressed in the teaching of Jesus Christ and the Holy Spirit within us powerfully reminds us of the standards set for us. Justice is not merely compliance with the law, but being just and honest in all our dealings, coupled with mercy shown to all our fellow human beings, whoever they are. It is about mutual respect, understanding and compassion.

We can only do this as we walk with God, humbly admitting our own need and frailty, 'trusting not in our own righteousness, but in his manifold and great mercy' (from the *Book of Common Prayer*) and then living it out in the same spirit with others.

Sunday reflection

What are we offering to the Lord today? Our presence in church, our involvement in worship, what we put on the plate? Is there something we might have forgotten? Let us ask ourselves the question 'With what shall I come before the Lord?' then remember his reply and do it.

MC

This is our God

Shepherd your people with your staff, the flock that belongs to you, which lives alone in a forest in the midst of a garden land; let them feed in Bashan and Gilead, as in the days of old. As in the days when you came out of the land of Egypt, show us marvellous things... Who is a God like you, pardoning iniquity and passing over the transgression of the remnant of your possession? He does not retain his anger for ever, because he delights in showing clemency. He will again have compassion upon us; he will tread our iniquities under foot. You will cast all our sins into the depths of the sea. You will show faithfulness to Jacob and unswerving loyalty to Abraham, as you have sworn to our ancestors from the days of old.

The people look back at their long history and what God has done for them. They do not look back wistfully, but in penitence and hope. They realize how he has cared for his people from the beginning, but also how they have turned away from him and fallen into sin. Like sheep they wandered, disobeyed, ignored their shepherd, but now they ask to be restored to the fold, brought back to the place God intended for them. There is hope for them, for now they realize their need and turn to the one who is the only source of help.

'Who is a God like you?' Who else can forgive and restore and delights to do so? We have the glorious picture of God joyfully crushing our sins, destroying their power, before throwing them into the sea, gone forever. Then he remakes us, gathering up the broken pieces of our lives and making us whole. Amazing grace indeed!

So we come to the end of our readings from Micah on that great note of thanksgiving and hope, the hope that would be fully realized in the coming of Jesus, God's gift to the world.

Prayer

Who is a God like you? We praise and thank you, God of power and might, that you have revealed yourself to us in Jesus Christ, that we can know the joy of sins forgiven and the power of your Holy Spirit, enabling us to walk in your ways as your people.

MC

Lord of power and might

The Lord is slow to anger but great in power, and the Lord will by no means clear the guilty. His way is in whirlwind and storm, and the clouds are the dust of his feet. He rebukes the sea and makes it dry, and he dries up all the rivers; Bashan and Carmel wither, and the bloom of Lebanon fades. The mountains quake before him, and the hills melt... Who can endure the heat of his anger? His wrath is poured out like fire, and by him the rocks are broken in pieces. The Lord is good, a stronghold on a day of trouble; he protects those who take refuge in him, even in a rushing flood.

'Prophecy requires saying things that are often uncomfortable, and often beautiful, and sometimes both.' I read those words in the leader column of my national daily newspaper just before going into my study to get to grips with the book of Nahum. I realized that the description of prophecy by a 21st-century journalist was a very apt summary of that book—uncomfortable and beautiful. Nahum reminds us of the awesome power of the almighty creator of heaven and earth, the Lord God, judge of all people. His words of prophecy tumble like poetry as he describes the power and majesty of God. He speaks of the fruitful and beautiful regions of Bashan, Carmel and Lebanon withering, consumed by the fire of God's visitation, the frightening forces of nature overcoming the pride and joy of human resources.

As we read the description of God's judgment on the Assyrians, a powerful nation, we are reminded that God is Lord of history. He is in control. He was from the beginning and he will be until the end, until he chooses to wind up history. Nothing and no one can withstand his power. That can make us very uncomfortable, for who are we to approach such a God? Yet the promise runs throughout scripture that those who turn to God and seek his forgiveness and grace will receive it, that his steadfast love is sure and certain and has been revealed for us in Jesus. He is our rock, our sure and certain hope for all eternity.

Prayer

Rock of ages, cleft for me,
let me hide myself in thee!

A.M. Toplady (1740–78)

MC

No escape

All your fortresses are like fig trees with first-ripe figs—if shaken they fall into the mouth of the eater. Look at your troops; they are women in your midst. The gates of your land are wide open to your foes… Draw water for the siege, strengthen your forts; trample the clay, tread the mortar, take hold of the brick mould! There the fire will devour you, the sword will cut you off. It will devour you like the locust. Multiply yourselves like the locust, multiply like the grasshopper! … Your guards are like grasshoppers, your scribes like swarms of locusts settling on the fences on a cold day—when the sun rises, they fly away; no one knows where they have gone.

What marvellous descriptive writing, creating cartoon pictures of the mighty Assyrians! It shows those so proud of their attack and defence systems being utterly destroyed, the city of Nineveh demolished. The prophecy has a teasing tone, but it is in deadly earnest and was fulfilled, as history reveals. Could anyone have imagined these events taking place when the Assyrians seemed to have total power? It would have taken more than imagination. It had to be revelation from the source beyond all powers and might on earth—that of God himself.

After the events were fulfilled, Nahum's words would be read in celebration as people looked back on what God had done. God had vanquished their enemies—how great was their God! Yet did they, or do we, really see that it was not God taking sides, but God being true to himself? Evil will always be put down, righteousness defended and justice will prevail, however strong the forces of corruption may appear. We may see ourselves as the 'goodies' and others as 'baddies', but what matters is how God sees and judges us. Nahum's picture of God's judgment evidenced in one time and place serves to remind us that we too stand under his judgment for the way we live our lives, both in relation to him and our fellows here and now.

Prayer

Lord, show me myself, in the light of your holiness and power. Grant me honesty and humility, that I may be saved from the pride of self-security to seek forgiveness and restoration in your mercy alone.

MC

First things first

Thus says the Lord of hosts: These people say the time has not yet come to rebuild the Lord's house. Then the word of the Lord came by the prophet Haggai, saying: Is it a time for you yourselves to live in your panelled houses, while this house lies in ruins? Now therefore, thus says the Lord of hosts: Consider how you have fared. You have sown much, and harvested little; you eat, but you never have enough; you drink, but you never have your fill; you clothe yourselves, but no one is warm; and you that earn wages earn wages to put them into a bag with holes. Thus says the Lord of hosts... Go up to the hills and bring wood and build the house, so that I may take pleasure in it, and be honoured, says the Lord.

What a relief it must have been for the exiles to return home at last and with permission to rebuild the temple. They returned with thankfulness and enthusiasm, but realized that it was going to be very hard work rebuilding their lives, homes, society. There were many setbacks. They struggled and yet they were getting nowhere. Rebuilding God's house was put on one side because there were far more important things to do, or so they thought. Time went by, apathy set in, promises were forgotten, but God has not forgotten and he speaks to the people through Haggai. It is a very direct message —a rebuke to his people and a challenge to them to look at what has happened. By putting themselves first before God, they have not gained anything. First things first, said God, build my house!

Maybe, as we look at life today, these words spoken to people long ago ring true for us. As the saying goes, we have to run to stand still. Has the Church been putting God first or its own concerns? How about ourselves—what are our priorities? What are we building? When God is put first, when he is honoured and obeyed, everything else falls into place.

Reflection and prayer

Jesus said, 'Strive first for the kingdom of God and his righteousness' (Matthew 6:33). Father, may you always be first in my heart, my mind and my actions.

MC

Take courage and build well

For thus says the Lord of hosts: Once again, in a little while, I will shake the heavens and the earth and the sea and the dry land; and I will shake all the nations, so that the treasure of all nations shall come, and I will fill this house with splendour, says the Lord of hosts. The silver is mine, and the gold is mine, says the Lord of hosts. The latter splendour of this house shall be greater than the former, says the Lord of hosts; and in this place I will give prosperity, says the Lord of hosts.

Do you remember the good old days when everybody was honest, when you could leave your door unlocked night and day? There was no shouting or swearing, the streets were clean, the sun shone every day. You could go to the pictures on a Saturday night, have a good fish and chip supper and still have change from a shilling, and all the churches were full every Sunday. Maybe or maybe not, but nostalgia does come complete with rose-tinted glasses and can hinder our getting on with life as it is today, blurring our vision for the future.

The exiles were now busy rebuilding the temple, but were very disheartened for they felt it would never be as glorious as Solomon's temple. Anyway, how could they obtain all the precious elements? Who would pay for it? God's word of encouragement is the promise that all the nations will come with offerings. There will be nothing lacking, for God is the Lord of hosts and everything belongs to him, including the gold and silver. Their job was to build and God would provide what was needed. With such encouragement, no wonder they went forward with vigour!

We are engaged in an even more glorious task—building God's kingdom—and what a wonderful celebration the completion day will be, when we see God face to face? In Revelation 21:22, we read, 'I saw no temple in the city, for its temple is the Lord God the Almighty and the Lamb.' What more encouragement do we need?

Reflection

Am I using the gifts God has given me to the best advantage? Whose plan am I working to, his or mine?

MC

HAGGAI 2:15–19 (NRSV, ABRIDGED)

The blessing of obedience

But now, consider what will come to pass from this day on. Before a stone was placed upon a stone in the Lord's temple, how did you fare? … I struck you and all the products of your toil with blight and mildew and hail; yet you did not return to me, says the Lord. Consider from this day on, from the 24th day of the 9th month. Since the day that the foundation of the Lord's temple was laid, consider: Is there any seed left in the barn? Do the vine, the fig tree, the pomegranate, and the olive tree still yield nothing? From this day on I will bless you.

The people have a new start, blessed by God for their faith and obedience. The past with its successes and failures, celebrations and mournings, was history. The people of God have moved on, no longer just returning exiles, focused on making a life for themselves out of the ruins. Now, having heeded God's word through his prophet Haggai and obeyed it, they have a new beginning, God's gift to them.

As we think about their story, let us remember the grace of God towards us in Christ Jesus. We have been brought back to God and our place in God's holy temple, the living temple. Read Ephesians 2:17–22 and try to take in what you have been rescued from, and what God has called you to be and enables you to be by virtue of his grace and power. Haggai was a faithful servant of God, who spoke God's word to the leaders and all the people, boldly, bravely and without compromise. Such prophets are thin on the ground in our generation, but 'the word of the Lord' is loud and clear for us in scripture, in God's living Word, his Son, and revealed to us by his Holy Spirit. It is our part to hear and obey, then we will enjoy his blessing.

Reflection and prayer

Long ago God spoke to our ancestors in many and various ways by the prophets, but in these last days he has spoken to us by a Son, whom he appointed heir of all things, through whom he also created the worlds (Hebrews 1:1–2).

Lord, may I build and be built for your praise and glory.

MC

Coping with criticism

After this, Jesus went around in Galilee, purposely staying away from Judea because the Jews there were waiting to take his life. But when the Jewish Feast of Tabernacles was near, Jesus' brothers said to him, 'You ought to leave here and go to Judea, so that your disciples may see the miracles you do. No one who wants to become a public figure acts in secret. Since you are doing these things, show yourself to the world.' For even his own brothers did not believe in him. Therefore Jesus told them, 'The right time for me has not yet come; for you any time is right... You go to the Feast. I am not yet going up to this Feast, because for me the right time has not yet come.' Having said this, he stayed in Galilee. However, after his brothers had left for the Feast, he went also, not publicly, but in secret.

Last spring, we left John's Gospel at the point when many of Jesus' disciples were deserting him and the religious leaders in Jerusalem were plotting to kill him. Back in Galilee, he encounters more hostility, this time from his own brothers who just cannot see him as the Son of God.

Those of us who find it difficult to cope with opposition can learn much from Jesus' example. He did not allow himself to feel put down, nor did he react aggressively. What was his secret? First, he was completely confident about who he was as Son of God and what he had to do on his Father's behalf. He also knew that he could only do this in his Father's way and according to his Father's timing.

Second, he was prepared for opposition. He was here to bring the kingdom of God to the people and was attacking some of the present-day systems and values as evil. If he went to the Feast of Tabernacles in Jerusalem he would go on his own terms, in God's time, which would be the right time for him to deliver God's message.

Sunday reflection

How do you cope with opposition within your church? Can you place it firmly in God's hands, wait for his guidance, do it his way and in his time?

CC

Listening to Jesus

About the middle of the festival Jesus went up into the temple and began to teach. The Jews were astonished at it, saying, 'How does this man have such learning, when he has never been taught?' Then Jesus answered them, 'My teaching is not mine but his who sent me. Anyone who resolves to do the will of God will know whether the teaching is from God or whether I am speaking on my own. Those who speak on their own seek their own glory; but the one who seeks the glory of him who sent him is true, and there is nothing false in him.'

The Feast of Tabernacles was the great Feast in the Jewish year celebrating both the harvest of that year and the goodness of God to the people of Moses' time during their desert wanderings. On this occasion, Jesus knew that God wanted him to go at a particular time, perhaps to avoid some of the leaders in Jerusalem and teach more of God's word to the people.

So, halfway through, when the crowds would be at their greatest, Jesus went on his own and taught in the temple courts. Most of those who went forward as teachers would have the authority of having studied under a recognized Jewish teacher. Most of them would be teaching various aspects of the law as given by Moses. Jesus had not studied under anyone—except his Father.

No wonder the people were amazed at hearing God's word spoken directly to them, with such authority. Jesus knew that those who listened to God, rather than about him in the law, would know the truth of his teaching. However, most of the leaders had a total focus on the law and could not believe that God would speak directly through a man like Jesus.

We Christians have our own mindsets, too, sometimes. I know that when I remember to ask Jesus for his wisdom, guidance, love and inspiration I am much more alive, sensitive and true to myself and others than when I go along in my own way with my own mindset. As God was Jesus' teacher, so may Jesus be ours.

Meditation

It is no longer I who live,
but it is Christ who lives in me.
(Galatians 2:20)

CC

JOHN 7:25–30 (NIV)

Rules or faith?

At that point some of the people of Jerusalem began to ask, 'Isn't this the man they are trying to kill? Here he is, speaking publicly, and they are not saying a word to him. Have the authorities really concluded that he is the Christ? But we know where this man is from; when the Christ comes, no one will know where he is from.' Then Jesus, still teaching in the temple courts, cried out, 'Yes, you know me, and you know where I am from. I am not here on my own, but he who sent me is true. You do not know him, but I know him because I am from him and he sent me.' At this they tried to seize him, but no one laid a hand on him, because his time had not yet come.

The people were just not into this kind of Christ or Messiah. The leaders in Jerusalem seemed to concentrate on what was written in the law rather than what was spoken by the prophets. Isaiah and others did prophesy about a Christ-like Jesus (see Isaiah 53), but the leaders liked laws and rules by which to live. So do most of us, if we are honest. They give us a tangible system of security, with standards that can be measured. Within the law, though, there is little room for surprises or the unpredictability of God.

Today, in the light of the New Testament, we can accept Jesus as Christ, in the sense of saviour, healer, sender of the Holy Spirit, giver of eternal life. However, we may still find it difficult to accept such values as those preached in the Sermon on the Mount. We find it quite unreasonable to love our enemies or even to accept the power of the Holy Spirit, which stretches us beyond human ability and understanding. Jesus left us with no set of rules and no security except faith in him. Yet, paradoxically, with that faith, we can transcend laws and human understanding and enter into the kingdom of God's love and mercy, of life lived to the full in the power of the Holy Spirit.

Reflection

'For my thoughts are not your thoughts, neither are your ways my ways,' declares the Lord.
(Isaiah 55:8)

CC

JOHN 7:31–36a (NIV)

The freedom of faith

Still, many in the crowd put their faith in him. They said, 'When the Christ comes, will he do more miraculous signs than this man?' The Pharisees heard the crowd whispering such things about him. Then the chief priests and the Pharisees sent temple guards to arrest him. Jesus said, 'I am with you for only a short time, and then I go to the one who sent me. You will look for me, but you will not find me; and where I am, you cannot come.' The Jews said to one another, 'Where does this man intend to go that we cannot find him? Will he go where our people live scattered among the Greeks, and teach the Greeks? What did he mean…?'

Jesus' absolute trust in his Father to govern his life—and death—shows us what real freedom is. He was not worried about being arrested before he had completed his work because the time of his arrest was in his Father's hands. He was not worried about what would happen when he died because he would be going back to the Father he came from and loved. He knew that the Jews could not accept his divine origin and therefore would never find him after his 'departure'. What he did show great concern for at the time was the manner of his death, when he would be cut off from his beloved Father. However, he knew he had to allow this to happen so that he could identify completely with us in our sin. Then, when God raised him up he would have the power to take us to the Father after our death.

We can see the freedom that is ours if we put our whole lives, and deaths, into the hands of God. What happens then is God's will for us; if not, we know we can trust Christ to redeem whatever goes wrong.

Meditation

'Do not let your hearts be troubled.
Trust in God; trust also in me…
If I go and prepare a place for you,
I will come back and take you to be
with me that you also may be where
I am. You know the way to the place
where I am going.'
(John 14:1, 3–4)

CC

Rivers of living water

On the last day of the festival, the great day, while Jesus was standing there, he cried out, 'Let anyone who is thirsty come to me, and let the one who believes in me drink. As the scripture has said, "Out of the believer's heart shall flow rivers of living water."' Now he said this about the Spirit, which believers in him were to receive; for as yet there was no Spirit, because Jesus was not yet glorified. When they heard these words, some in the crowd said, 'This is really the prophet.' Others said, 'This is the Messiah.'

Jesus was given his message by his Father. Teachers usually sat, so standing up and crying out in a loud voice would certainly attract attention to what he was saying. The subject of water would be on everyone's minds because on the last day of the festival there was a procession with water from Siloam to the temple. During the water ceremony people sang, 'With joy you will draw water from the wells of salvation…' (Isaiah 12:3). The water was not actually drunk, but was taken up to the temple. Now, Jesus said, the believer can drink the water of salvation from him. Then the water becomes a river in his heart by the power of the Spirit.

Some felt that Jesus was more than the prophet from Galilee, that he was in fact the Christ. People believe for different reasons. The river of living water flowing from within has always struck a chord with me. Believing in Jesus is a two-way relationship. As we pray to him in love and trust, we may be aware of Jesus reaching out and touching our hearts, making himself known to us in his Spirit. Once we accept the gift of the Holy Spirit and enter into a living relationship with Christ, we have truly found Christ as our salvation, as the answer to our longings, as our life-giving friend.

Prayer

Jesus, grant that I may be aware of you as I pray and at all times, listening to me lovingly. Grant that I may pause and soak in your love, that I may hear what you are saying, that I may allow your Spirit to touch my heart and restore and renew me.

CC

The courage to face ridicule

Finally the temple guards went back to the chief priests and Pharisees, who asked them, 'Why didn't you bring him in?' 'No one ever spoke the way this man does', the guards declared. 'You mean he has deceived you, also?' the Pharisees retorted. 'Has any of the rulers or of the Pharisees believed in him? No! But this mob that knows nothing of the law—there is a curse on them.' Nicodemus, who had gone to Jesus earlier and who was one of their own number, asked, 'Does our law condemn a man without first hearing him to find out what he is doing?' They replied, 'Are you from Galilee, too? Look into it, and you will find that a prophet does not come out of Galilee.'

This confrontational scene between the Pharisees and the temple guards reflects the kinds of feelings that Jesus evoked. The Pharisees were furious with the guards for not seizing Jesus and the guards were too impressed by Jesus to lay a finger on him. So, the Pharisees tried to ridicule the guards and devalue the ordinary people's knowledge of the law. No one of any standing, they intimated, believed in Jesus.

However, there was one person of high social standing who had shown great interest in Jesus—Nicodemus, a member of the Jewish ruling council, who had made a secret visit to Jesus at night. He was prepared to tackle the other Pharisees on their own ground by pointing out that they were not keeping to the law either if they condemned Jesus without a trial. Then it was Nicodemus' turn to be called ignorant of the scriptures. We do not know if Nicodemus replied that at least one prophet, Jonah, had actually come out of Galilee or that Isaiah mentions Galilee in his prophesies about the coming Messiah (Isaiah 9:1).

Jesus was breaking through by opening up some people's hearts. Some went on to make that wholehearted commitment to him that gave them the courage and love not only to stand up to ridicule, but also to die for him rather than deny their faith.

Prayer

Jesus, give me the courage to stand up for my beliefs when challenged and the will to deepen my commitment by regular prayer and worship.

CC

Rules or mercy?

At dawn he appeared again in the temple courts, where all the people gathered round him, and he sat down to teach them. The teachers of the law and the Pharisees brought in a woman caught in adultery. They made her stand before the group and said to Jesus, 'Teacher, this woman was caught in the act of adultery. In the Law Moses commanded us to stone such women. Now what do you say?' They were using this question as a trap, in order to have a basis for accusing him. But Jesus bent down and started to write on the ground with his finger. When they kept on questioning him, he straightened up and said to them, 'If any one of you is without sin, let him be the first to throw a stone at her.'

It was a pretty dramatic interruption to Jesus' teaching session. Was he controlling his anger as he remained silent and wrote on the ground? He did not challenge the Pharisees on their outrageous action; neither did he tell them they were misrepresenting the law anyway (Deuteronomy 22:23–24). He turned it all into another teaching point: were the Pharisees always completely without sin that they felt able to judge the woman in this way? Was not God's love and mercy needed by all alike, whether or not some kept parts of the law better than others?

It is a difficult point for those who like rules. Three children in my family were once playing a boardgame and were persuaded to let their younger brother join in, though he did not understand all the rules. He was thrilled, but then became upset when he could not get the right colour on the dice even to begin. The eldest child said, 'Let's pretend you've got the white and then you can go on', but her younger sister was furious. She was not above cheating herself but in this case she was both winning and obeying the rules. 'That's not fair. Mum, she's breaking the rules. That's cheating.' Mum tried her best, but the six-year-old could not yet see that love could be a more praiseworthy quality than righteousness according to rules.

Reflection

'Blessed are the merciful,
for they will be shown mercy.'
(Matthew 5:7)

CC

The light of the world—in us

When Jesus spoke again to the people, he said, 'I am the light of the world. Whoever follows me will never walk in darkness, but will have the light of life.' The Pharisees challenged him, 'Here you are, appearing as your own witness; your testimony is not valid.' Jesus answered, 'Even if I testify on my own behalf, my testimony is valid, for I know where I came from and where I am going... You judge by human standards... I stand with the Father, who sent me. In your own Law it is written that the testimony of two men is valid. I am one who testifies for myself; my other witness is the Father, who sent me.'

As many Christians find some of Jesus' teachings hard, it is not surprising that the Jewish leaders found them unacceptable. Light, like water, was a Jewish image of salvation, as depicted in the ceremony of light at the Feast of Tabernacles, but Jesus is saying, 'I am the light' or, in other words, 'I am the bringer of salvation.' What a claim! Unless this man from Nazareth was divine, he could not possibly validate his claims. How, humanly speaking, could he be divine? So the arguments between Jesus and the Pharisees went on.

I think many Christians would be hard put to say with conviction that they had the 'light of life'. Yet that is what Jesus is saying we have if we follow him. Again and again, Jesus speaks of the necessity of our 'eating' him as the bread of life, 'drinking him' as living water, 'living in us' and us 'living in him'. He asks us to receive him into our very selves so that we have his Spirit, the Holy Spirit, dwelling in us as part of our nature.

If we truly follow Jesus, the light of the world, we will have his light in us, but it may shine dimly through our busyness, emotions, our own agendas. If we want to shine more clearly, maybe we have to ask Jesus to help us clear all the clouds in the way.

Sunday reflection

Could you be a light in your church, reflecting Jesus' light from within you to those around you?

CC

Father—Abba

Then they asked him, 'Where is your father?' 'You do not know me or my Father,' Jesus replied. 'If you knew me, you would know my Father also.' ... But he continued, 'You are from below; I am from above. You are of this world; I am not of this world. I told you that you would die in your sins; if you do not believe that I am the one I claim to be, you will indeed die in your sins.' 'Who are you?' they asked. 'Just what I have been claiming all along,' Jesus replied... 'When you have lifted up the Son of Man, then you will know that I am the one I claim to be and that I do nothing on my own but speak just what the Father has taught me.'

One of the most moving parts of the Passion Play at Oberammergau for me was the sight and sound of Jesus talking, appealing, crying out to his Father. Somehow, the term, 'God' would have been too remote. It was always 'Father', in its most affectionate, intimate form. The relationship between Jesus and God was the most perfect relationship that a human being could ever have with God, because of their heavenly oneness before the world ever began. The Pharisees were not against the concept of God as Father, but they were against Jesus' view of him as 'Daddy'. We learn later in John's Gospel that Jesus wanted all those who believed in him to have this same close, loving relationship with God—in him.

'Who are you?' they asked. Jesus often called himself Son of Man as a messianic title, probably referring to the vision of Daniel (7:13–14). He uses the term 'lifted up' to mean crucifixion, though not everyone would understand this. Jesus had to wait until after his resurrection before people could understand more fully who he was. In the meantime, he had to prepare the people, knowing that those whose views were limited to this world could never accept his claims and so have a more open prayer relationship with God.

Reflection

Do you think of God in a close, loving way, as well as being aware of him as the Almighty Creator God of heaven and earth?

CC

The truth will set you free

To the Jews who had believed him, Jesus said, 'If you hold to my teaching, you are really my disciples. Then you will know the truth, and the truth will set you free.' They answered him, 'We are Abraham's descendants and have never been slaves of anyone. How can you say that we shall be set free?' Jesus replied, 'I tell you the truth, everyone who sins is a slave to sin. Now a slave has no permanent place in the family, but a son belongs to it for ever. So if the Son sets you free, you will be free indeed.'

Jesus is now teaching those who have professed faith in him so far. They are just beginning the journey of faith, possibly drawn to him because of his miracles and healings. Now he stretches them further, to what he has been teaching, the truth that will set them free, but the stretching seems too much for them. They were free already, weren't they? Jesus was teaching completely new ideas about the nature of sin, their relationship with God, the nature of God himself. As usual, his teaching was misunderstood or taken literally, on earthly terms rather than spiritual terms. As usual, they began to ask questions. Sometimes, as Jesus answered questions, some would begin to understand. In this passage, Jesus' teaching points primarily to himself, as the one sent by God to speak his words. We have seen him refer to himself as the bread of life, living water, the light of the world, giver of eternal life.

Now he is the Son who sets them free from the slavery of sin.

I wonder how many of his hearers began to question their claim to a right relationship with God on account of their perceived position as his chosen people through Abraham. It required a complete U-turn to start looking at their personal state of sin and then look to Jesus as the Son of God who could free them to have a new relationship with God.

Prayer

Jesus Christ, my Lord and Saviour, grant me the courage to look at my own personal sins, the grace to repent, the humility to ask forgiveness and the joy of accepting freedom in your name.

CC

JOHN 8:42–47 (NIV, ABRIDGED)

Belonging to God

Jesus said to them, 'If God were your Father, you would love me, for I came from God and now am here. I have not come on my own; but he sent me. Why is my language not clear to you? Because you are unable to hear what I say. You belong to your father, the devil, and you want to carry out your father's desire... Yet because I tell the truth, you do not believe me! Can any of you prove me guilty of sin? If I am telling the truth, why don't you believe me? He who belongs to God hears what God says. The reason you do not hear is that you do not belong to God.'

Can you imagine Jesus looking at one person, then another, as he makes these damning statements and asks these difficult questions? They could not answer. They knew that they did not have that father–child relationship with God that Jesus was talking about. Neither did they really want to believe in him, for that would threaten their security. However, there must have been something very compelling about Jesus as he was teaching.

Then he went too far, accusing them of belonging to the devil rather than God. That sounds outrageous, yet we could say that it was the power of evil that drove the leaders to condemn Jesus to death. The more followers he acquired—mostly uneducated people—the more threatened they felt and the more devious were their plans to kill him. The trouble was that they could not prove him guilty of sin.

Neither, of course, could Jesus prove that he was the Son of God. They just had to believe in the person of Jesus drawing them to him, with his love and healing for those who knew their need for God.

It is not much different for us, though we are further on in our understanding of Jesus. We are first and foremost drawn to him as the Son of God, the risen Christ. Then, in the light of the living relationship he offers us, we come to know God as our Father and that we truly belong.

Prayer

Risen Lord, draw me to yourself and turn my face towards you.

CC

'In the beginning was the Word...'

'I tell you the truth, if anyone keeps my word, he will never see death.' At this the Jews exclaimed, 'Now we know that you are demon-possessed! Abraham died and so did the prophets, yet you say that if anyone keeps your word, he will never taste death. Are you greater than our father Abraham?... Who do you think you are?' Jesus replied, 'If I glorify myself, my glory means nothing. My Father, whom you claim as your God, is the one who glorifies me... Your father Abraham rejoiced at the thought of seeing my day; he saw it and was glad.' 'You are not yet 50 years old,' the Jews said to him, 'and you have seen Abraham!' 'I tell you the truth,' Jesus answered, 'before Abraham was born, I am!'

'I am'—the name God told Moses to call him when he revealed himself in the burning bush (Exodus 3:14). Yes, Jesus is greater than Abraham. He was with God in the beginning, the Word, the true light that gives light to everyone. He is claiming his divinity in no uncertain terms. Well, they asked him who he thought he was and he told them. Many years ago, when I was struggling to establish what I really believed—and getting nowhere—I read this passage and something 'clicked' inside me (it does happen sometimes, so take heart, if you are struggling). I 'knew' that Jesus really is the Son of God. Of course, it was blasphemy to the Jews and that was the end of it for many of them, but for those of us who seek to know Jesus for ourselves, it is the beginning. Jesus is human and divine.

He understands us. He is the Son of God, and the Man without sin who has the power to forgive us for our sins. He is the bridge spanning the distance between us on earth and our Father in heaven—always available, always approachable. He gives us 'eternal life', a new quality of life experienced by knowing Jesus, both here and now and after our death, too, though in a fuller, more perfect way, of course. Jesus is Lord!

Prayer

Jesus, grant me such a knowledge of you that I may worship you with all my heart as my Lord.

CC

Is God punishing me?

As he went along, he saw a man blind from birth. His disciples asked him, 'Rabbi, who sinned, this man or his parents, that he was born blind?' 'Neither this man nor his parents sinned,' said Jesus, 'but this happened so that the work of God might be displayed in his life. As long as it is day, we must do the work of him who sent me. Night is coming, when no one can work. While I am in the world, I am the light of the world.' Having said this, he spat on the ground, made some mud with the saliva, and put it on the man's eyes. 'Go,' he told him, 'wash in the Pool of Siloam' (this word means Sent). So the man went and washed, and came home seeing.

How often do you hear people say, when they are suffering, 'What have I done wrong to deserve this?' or even, 'God must be punishing me.' The Jewish rabbis promoted the theory that suffering is God's punishment for wickedness and even children's suffering may have been because of the wickedness of their parents. In fact, the second commandment, forbidding the worship of idols, warns that God punishes children for the sin of their fathers to the third and fourth generation (Exodus 20:5). Jesus is having none of this punishment theory, however, and concentrates rather on God's way of transforming difficult situations.

At the Feast of Tabernacles, the 'water of salvation' was brought from the Pool of Siloam and John's note about the word meaning 'sent' implies that Jesus, sent from God, was also in the water with his power to save. While Jesus was in the world, he healed people in many ways, often physically, as an outward sign of inner healing or salvation. Now, as the risen Lord, he is still the light of the world and heals and saves in the Holy Spirit. As those indwelt with the Spirit, it is surely up to us to shine his light of love and compassion in the darkness of people's suffering and, with prayer, begin his process of transformation and healing.

Prayer

Lord, grant me the faith to know your transforming light in my own darkness and to spread it in the darkness around me.

CC

Challenge

They brought to the Pharisees the man who had been blind. Now the day on which Jesus had made the mud and opened the man's eyes was a Sabbath... Some of the Pharisees said, 'This man is not from God, for he does not keep the Sabbath.' But others asked, 'How can a sinner do such miraculous signs?' So they were divided. Finally they turned again to the blind man, 'What have you to say about him? It was your eyes he opened.' The man replied, 'He is a prophet.' ... A second time they summoned the man who had been blind. 'Give glory to God,' they said, 'We know this man is a sinner.' He replied, 'Whether he is a sinner or not, I don't know. One thing I do know. I was blind but now I see!'

The Pharisees were clearly perplexed and divided in their opinions by this miracle, so they turned to the blind man himself, which was unusual. He abandoned all arguments about the Sabbath and whether or not Jesus was a sinner. He stated simply what he did know, which was that once he was blind, but now he could see.

I attended a course for Christians about the Muslim religion and part of the course was a visit to a mosque, led by an Asian Christian. Outside the mosque we met a youth on a motorbike, who stopped beside us and engaged us in conversation, asking why we had come. We started to say that we were interested in finding out more about the Muslim religion and were taken aback by his firm response: 'Your Jesus, we believe in him too, but he was not the Son of God—that is impossible.' While we struggled for words, torn between wanting to be courteous and defending our faith, our leader quietly stepped forward, put his hand on the youth's shoulder, and said, 'My friend, I know that Jesus is the Son of God. I know.' With a simple statement, our leader had kept his integrity as a Christian and said what he knew, with love. There was no answer to that—true faith transcends argument. Let us be confident about what we believe in our hearts, whether or not we can prove it.

Prayer
Lord, I believe. Help me to know.

CC

Open our eyes, Lord

The man answered [the Pharisees], 'Now that is remarkable! You don't know where he comes from, yet he opened my eyes. We know that God does not listen to sinners. He listens to the godly man who does his will. Nobody has ever heard of opening the eyes of a man born blind. If this man were not from God, he could do nothing.' To this they replied, 'You were steeped in sin at birth; how dare you lecture us!' And they threw him out. Jesus heard that they had thrown him out, and when he found him, he said, 'Do you believe in the Son of Man?' 'Who is he, sir?' the man asked. 'Tell me so that I may believe in him.' Jesus said, 'You have now seen him; in fact, he is the one speaking with you.' Then the man said, 'Lord, I believe,' and he worshipped him.

What was going on in that man's mind as he saw the world around him for the first time? He was convinced that Jesus, who had enabled him to see, must be from God. Then Jesus came to him again and invited him to see yet further, to see that the Son of Man, the Messiah, was standing before him. The man saw, believed and worshipped Jesus as God.

At last someone comes to full belief in Jesus Christ, after all the disbelief and criticisms we have encountered in these readings. It is when we acknowledge Jesus as Lord that the 'scales fall from our eyes' and we are opened to a new world—the kingdom of God. We see everything with new eyes. We see God as our loving Father; we see the world as created and belonging to God, we dare to look at and face our failings, knowing that Jesus will take them in hand and redeem them. We look on our bodies and souls as indwelt by the Holy Spirit, the living water of Christ, and we see our whole lives in an eternal light, seeing death as the beginning of a new life.

Sunday reflection

Have our eyes been opened to 'believe in one Lord, Jesus Christ, the only Son of God… God from God, Light from Light…'?

From the Nicene Creed

CC

New Daylight

Magazine

Deadlines and lifelines

Russ Bravo

Society is dying, and the media's to blame. Society is dying, and the Church is to blame—because it's failed to communicate the greatest story ever told. Russ Bravo delves into the vexed issue of the Church and the media.

I've worked in the media for more than 22 years, 21 of them as a committed, believing Christian. I've never been more excited about the opportunities that are opening up for Christians these days—and I've never been more depressed by the blinkered, one-dimensional, feckless attitude that God's people all too often have when it comes to the media.

Let me explain a little. A simple equation might put it this way: gospel = good news; media = bad news. Conclusion: the two cannot mix. The media world is so corrupt and so clearly controlled by the enemy, Christians should have nothing to do with it. They shouldn't bother with such worldly things as newspapers and magazines, and they certainly shouldn't look to work within it.

'But that's not me!' you protest. Good, and my rather extreme summary would be unfair on many believers today. But the attitude is one that has been slow to change over the years, and when we com-plain bitterly about the national press, TV and radio, we must concede that the Church's past attitudes have been at least partly to blame. We have shied away from engagement with the media, fearful of being misrepresented, unwilling to get involved with something tainted with the world. At the same time, we have neglected to communicate effectively with the people we are trying to reach.

Also, those of us who pride ourselves on being 'Bible-based' have failed to learn from God's word, because good journalists and faithful disciples of Jesus actually have a lot in common:

- Both should have a passion for finding out and communicating truth.
- Both should have a love for people and the stories of their lives.
- Both should be determined to represent the world as it is to the people who live in it.
- Both believe in the power of words and images. Jesus used

parables and stories earthed in the society he was part of.

- Both need to understand how people tick.

God's hacks and presenters

The Bible tells us that God is constantly seeking to communicate with us. He has to work hard to get our attention a lot of the time. But then God's people have always been 'stiff-necked' and 'hard-hearted', so visual aids have often been pretty spectacular—not tabloids but tablets of stone, pillars of fire, burning bushes and the parting of the Red Sea.

We've had God's town criers—the prophets. Delivering God's message, they've been stoned, imprisoned, chucked down wells, swallowed by large fish and generally given a hard time.

How about John the Baptist? Preparing the way for Jesus, he was rewarded with decapitation. Then we have four journalists, Matthew, Mark, Luke and John, piecing together their accounts of Jesus' life and ministry, each bringing a different flavour, different sources and quotes. And of course Paul, the Bible's most provocative columnist—absolutely unmissable missives for the early Church that really put the cat among the pigeons.

Also, crucially, take a look at the way Jesus taught the crowds. If his teachings were published in newspaper format (and they have been, over the years) they would certainly have educated, informed and entertained his readers. He spoke with an intimate understanding of his audience, he had an economy with words, yet he connected with his listeners. He was passionate about sharing the truth with people—about God, and about themselves. He held a mirror up to them and said, 'Here, this is what you look like to God. And this is what God is like.'

The Church's choice

The media are among the biggest influences on our lives in the 21st century—TV, radio, film, magazines, newspapers, the internet, text messaging. We are bombarded by news, spin and images, and they do affect they way we think, the opinions we hold and the way we live.

Truth is one of the biggest casualties: it's not always the things that are said or written that are misleading, but the things that are left out. Debates on TV and radio are skewed to provide the most entertaining listening or viewing, not to shed light on important issues. You might know that one of the most important factors for radio presenters dealing in current affairs is 'conflict'—setting up two opposing spokespeople to shout each

> *God is constantly seeking to communicate*

other down on air. It brings little enlightenment, but it sure is fun to listen to.

So where does the Church stand in all this? There are three options. First, **do nothing**—what difference could we make anyway? We can continue to do what we do, building relationships with people locally, and not worry about the media. The problem with this is that we have to communicate somehow, and if we ignore all the current channels of communication, we make life very hard for ourselves. We also shrug off our duty to be a purifying and Christ-loving influence in our world. The general public may not like the media's approach either, but if they are not shown a better way, or given living, breathing examples of good journalism, good radio, good TV and good websites, then opportunities will continue to go begging.

Second, **retreat** into our own dedicated media channels—Christian radio, Christian TV, Christian publications. We're talking to ourselves, but at least it's not the world's way. This is a very tempting approach, and you'd expect me to be quite defensive about specifically Christian forms of media. After all, that's where I earn my crust at the moment. But I really believe that if the Church had engaged properly with the media world over the past 40 years, many of our Christian media channels would simply be unnecessary.

It's fine to have means of communicating with each other, and there is a limited place for our own newspapers, magazines, radio and TV stations. But when you look at the cost, particularly of radio, TV and websites, and consider that so many of these ventures constantly struggle to meet costs, and generally preach to the converted, you tend to feel—at least I do—that there must be a better way.

A land that needs inhabiting by Christians

Where are the pioneering believers producing great publications and programmes that catch the eyes and ears of those outside the Church?

Third, we could try **engagement**—and that's where my heart lies. The media world is a land that needs inhabiting by Christians. The whole history of the Church is about incarnation—God coming down among us. Jesus sent his disciples out, and later prayed, 'Do not take them out of the world.' Our role is to be salt and light in the dark places of society. The early Church was born into opposition, being at risk and in danger. Jesus left them, saying, 'In this world, you will have trouble—but take heart, I have overcome the world.'

It's not going to be easy, but our calling is not to an attitude that doesn't care and leaves us burying our heads in the sand. It's not even a calling to set up all our own things with a Christian label on and an audience of the faithful. It's surely to get our hands dirty and get among the people who need to know the love and forgiveness of God most urgently.

So when people come to me and say God's called them to be a Christian journalist, I usually respond, 'I doubt it.' God may have called you to be a journalist, but the mainstream media needs your presence as a Christian far more than we do. Go there. Get trained. Earn your crust. Be faithful to Jesus and be brilliant in your work. Climb the ladder—get into positions of influence.

If enough young believers went into the media with a twofold commitment to Christ and to being the best journalist or radio presenter or TV writer who ever lived, what a difference it would make!

Then the media surely would be good news.

Mainstream contacts

• National Council for the Training of Journalists: 01279 430009; www.nctj.com
• Broadcast Journalism Training Council: 020 7727 9522; www.bjtc.co.uk
• Periodicals Training Council: 020 7404 4168; www.ppa.co.uk

You can do undergraduate courses, postgrad courses, block release, day release, distance learning and many other kinds of courses at many colleges and universities across the UK.

Christian contacts

• uk-journalist: an e-mail discussion list for UK journalists who are Christians. Join by e-mailing: subscribe-uk-journalist@mail. icmc.org
• Gegrapha: global fellowship of Christians in journalism. Has an active group in the UK. Go to www.gegrapha.org
• International Christian Media Commission: www.icmc.org
• Books: *Christ and the Media* by Malcolm Muggeridge (try second-hand bookshops); *24 Lead Soldiers* by Dan Wooding (Kingsway): testimony/personal ministry of Dan Wooding, long-standing *Christian Herald* contributor and journalist, founder of ASSIST Ministries.

Other ministries worth checking out (more broadcasting-based):
• CACLB (Churches' Advisory Council on Local Broadcasting, soon to become the Churches' Media Council): 01245 322079; www.caclb.org.uk
• Arts Centre Group: 020 7243 4550; www.artscentregroup.org.uk

Russ Bravo is editor of Christian Herald, *the UK's only inter-church weekly newspaper, and editorial director of Christian Media Centre. He lives in Sussex with his wife and three children, and has worked as a journalist in local, regional and national newspapers since 1981.*

Christian bookshops—serving the church

Karen Laister

It was a book that led me into Christian bookselling and later into publishing—Edward England's *An Unfading Vision*. It spoke to me of the way in which God uses the Christian book ministry to equip people and the church for discipleship and growth. It was a book that not only inspired me but also gave me passion and vision to pursue a career in this ministry.

How often have you been challenged by a Christian book? Maybe you became a Christian after reading a book, or your faith has been renewed and refreshed when going through a desert experience, or you have found comfort during a time of personal anxiety through a book that offers words of comfort. Then there are theological and academic books that inform and teach, challenging us at both an intellectual and practical level.

There are around 600 Christian bookshops in the UK, and BRF books are also available in a number of Christian bookstores overseas. We are incredibly fortunate in the UK to have such a large number of shops and selection of Christian books and other media available on our doorstep. We know from the letters BRF receives from people in the developing world that they would love to have such a resource and to be able to buy the variety and depth of literature that is available to us. However, any Christian bookshop manager would tell you that very few Christians visit their shop and buy books.

Christian bookshops are there to serve the local community. They often provide a Christian witness on a busy high street. Some have a coffee shop to welcome those who want a haven from shopping or the general busyness of life. As well as welcoming customers to browse, some shops also work closely with churches providing bookstalls or books for special events like Advent fairs. Many shops have developed their businesses to enable people to purchase through mail order or through the Internet, adapting to the changing needs of customers today. Others organize events for authors and teaching days using a number of authors, artists and storytellers. BRF has worked with a number of booksellers helping to resource these types of events.

Visiting a bookshop can be an unhurried experience in which you can browse to your heart's content. It is also a tangible, tactile experience, allowing you to see and handle the books before you buy—something that an online bookshop cannot offer.

Not only offering the latest bestsellers, the shop will also present a range of subject areas with books reflecting a variety of Christian tradition. There has recently been an explosion in contemporary and traditional hymn recordings, which can be used for individual listening or worship, or even group worship. So a Christian bookshop is a rich resource that brings together Christians from across the breadth of the Church.

A Christian bookshop is a rich resource

A Christian bookshop is also an ideal place for buying presents for people, whether it is a gift for a new Christian or someone being baptized or confirmed, for Christmas or birthdays—you will find a huge selection of ideas.

If your church doesn't have a bookstall, why not consider organizing one? A bookshop manager will help you with the selection of stock and be able to offer advice about promoting the bookstall. They will also be able to provide magazines, articles and display posters.

Some shops welcome volunteer help, from serving customers to unpacking boxes. If you have some free time, why not drop in and offer?

A fun way to enjoy books is in a reading group. A number of secular bookshops organize such groups. They are not only a good way to meet people but they provide the opportunity to debate books which are particularly topical or which present a range of Christian views on a subject. (A good example is a book like BRF's *Faith Odyssey* by Richard Burridge, which looks at parallels between biblical literature and modern culture.) The book selected for discussion is read before the meeting, which takes place monthly or less frequently, depending on the members. Your local Christian bookshop may hold reading groups or be able to facilitate one.

So often, because of demands on our time, we forget about the people or things that are most important to us. All too often we are so immersed in day-to-day living that we neglect time to be quiet, to think and read about our faith. Over the next few weeks, why not take time to visit your local Christian bookshop? If you can't get to it, try browsing the bookstall in your church. You never know— you may end up choosing a book that changes your life, as *An Unfading Vision* did for me!

An extract from
(Extra)Ordinary Women

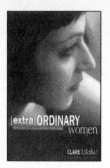

Subtitled 'Reflections for women on Bible-based living', this book is for all those who have ever felt that women in the Bible were superstars, somehow extra specially blessed by God. In a series of down-to-earth Bible reflections, based around the central theme that all women are special in God's eyes, it relates scripture teaching to everyday experience and shows how God has a special gifting for everyone. It is Clare Blake's first book although she has also written for *Wholeness, Woman Alive, Home and Family* and *Christian Herald*.

She was just an ordinary woman until he came on the scene
And his love showed her all that she was meant to be.
He knew all about her, every weakness, every strength,
But that just made him love her even more,
Especially when she tried to change and grow for his sake.
Each day she learned a little more about him
And trusted him a little more,
Learned to follow where he led
And listen when he spoke.
Learned to see herself not just as part of the wallpaper
But a living stone created for a purpose,
Unique because that was the way God had designed her
And only she could fill the special place prepared for her.
No longer ordinary, but extraordinary in him
Because that was how he was
And something of him now shone in her.

Doing it my way!

Short cuts are great when they work, but when they don't they can be frustrating, time-consuming, even downright dangerous. I well remember one walk on which we thought we would save a significant amount of time and energy by taking a different route to the marked footpath.

At first, all went well and progress was rapid, but soon we found ourselves negotiating a stretch of marshland, picking our way gingerly from tussock to tussock, occasionally missing our footing and sinking ankle-deep into rust-brown water. The clouds of mosquitoes buzzing round our heads didn't help matters either!

Although the road we were attempting to reach could be seen from where we stood, it took ages before we finally reached the comfort of its hard metalled surface. By this time our feet were soaked and tempers were short. 'Why on earth didn't we stick to the proper path?' Why indeed?

Before Abraham left Ur at the age of 75, God had promised, 'I will make of you a great nation' (Genesis 12:2). Four chapters later, however, and Abraham is beginning to get a bit worried. After all, he and Sarah aren't getting any younger. Anxiously he reminds God of his promise: 'O Lord God, what will you give me, for I continue childless, and the heir of my house is Eliezer of Damascus?' (Genesis 15:2).

Once again God reassures him, 'Your very own issue shall be your heir' (Genesis 15:4). He takes Abraham outside and shows him the night sky, promising that one day Abraham's offspring will be as numerous as the stars sprinkled in the heavens. Comforted, Abraham believes that God will do as he has said.

For Sarah, however, it's a slightly different story. She is very much aware of her biological clock ticking away. Where is the son that God has promised? Perhaps Abraham misunderstood what God had said.

Have you ever found yourself in a similar predicament? Waiting is terribly difficult. You believe you've clearly heard God speak but nothing in your situation seems to be changing. As days, months and even years pass by, you wonder what on earth is going on. Perhaps you feel that God has promised you a husband but it hasn't happened yet and you're getting tired of waiting for the right man. Or you were sure that God had promised you healing but the old aches and pains are just as bad.

The old serpent rears its ugly head once again: 'Has God said…?' Did he really say it or have we just been kidding ourselves all along? Is there perhaps another interpretation? Does it really matter how the promise comes about? Perhaps God wants us to use our own initiative.

Sarah couldn't bear the waiting any longer, so, like many of us, she decided to take matters into her own hands. She persuaded Abraham to take Hagar her maid as a wife-perhaps this would result in the longed-for baby. Hagar did become pregnant with Abraham's child, but, far from bringing joy, the successful outcome of Sarah's carefully planned strategy resulted in nothing but grief and jealousy when Hagar began to despise her barren mistress (Genesis 16:4).

In one sense, Sarah's plotting had been successful. She got what she wanted, but instead of bringing blessing it brought friction—friction that continues to this day in the strife between Israeli and Arab nations.

What would have happened if Sarah had waited for God to act, if she hadn't seized matters into her own hands? She would have saved Abraham and herself a lot of unnecessary grief. Trying to 'organize' God never works, as Sarah found out to her cost. In fact, it wasn't until, humanly speaking, all hope of a baby for Abraham and Sarah was long gone that God resolved their situation and fulfilled the promise he had given Abraham so many years ago.

When Sarah overheard the Lord saying that she would bear a son, her first reaction was incredulous laughter (Genesis 18:12), but she learned an important lesson in the long years of waiting. Sarah knew that she had already tried to fulfil the promise through her own efforts and that she had failed miserably. She knew that she and Abraham could do nothing about it on their own. By this time she had learnt wisdom. She knew that she had to step back and let God be God, to trust him and ignore the doubts.

She had to step back and let God be God

I wonder how Sarah felt when the baby stirred in her womb. Did she think, 'What a fool I was not to trust God in the first place! Why on earth did I run ahead of his plans for me?' Abraham's and Sarah's faith was rewarded by the birth of Isaac, whose name means 'laughter'. When we give our situations, however difficult, over to God and leave them in his hands, he brings joy into our lives.

We would like everything to be cut and dried, but God doesn't work like that. Sometimes prayers are answered immediately. At other times we grow weary because the answer seems so long in coming. Do not give up: persevere. God's timing is not our timing. God's timing is perfect.

To order a copy of this book, please turn to the order form on page 159.

An extract from
On This Rock

Author and evangelist Stephen Cottrell has written this book for new Christians who want to grow in their faith and for more experienced Christians who want to re-set the compass of their discipleship. In 28 Bible readings telling the story of the apostle Peter, he explores what being a disciple meant back then, and how it relates to the life of a disciple today. Stephen is one of the authors of *Emmaus; The Way of Faith*, a programme for evangelism, nurture and discipleship that is now used by about 3000 churches in Britain and around the world.

Greatness

We live in a society that exalts celebrity. Our newspapers are full of the latest gossip about the lives of pop stars and soap stars. The natural desire to do well and to do one's best is sometimes overtaken by the selfish desire to get on at the expense of others, to stand alone in the spotlight and receive the adulation of others. Very few of us have not dreamed about wealth and riches and fame. Why else would so many lottery tickets be sold each week? Why else are television quiz shows that offer huge financial rewards, or 'docu-soaps' that offer fifteen minutes of fame, so hugely popular?

…Christian vocation is hard because it requires us to put God first. We still love ourselves, but we love ourselves for God's sake, and in so doing learn proper love and respect for everyone.

Building Christian character involves chiselling out those self-centred attitudes that harden the human heart. It usually takes a long time. To be exact, it takes a lifetime. But by happy coincidence that is exactly how much time each of us has got!

In Mark 9:33–37 we find the disciples, Peter among them, arguing over who will be the greatest. They have been with Jesus for some time now, and seen his incredible effect in people's lives—his power to heal, his strength in facing opposition, his wisdom. They sense that he is the chosen one from God, and they start to dream of an earthly kingdom where he is the head. Now they wonder which of them will share this greatness. And Peter, no doubt, always a natural leader in the group, is probably advancing his claims.

Jesus comes alongside them. He knows what they are arguing about, but when he asks them to tell him they are shamed into silence. Jesus sits them down. 'Whoever wants to be first must be last of all and servant of all,' he says to them.

This is a hard saying. It goes against the grain of our desire to be important and well thought of and successful. We have to put others first. Our character will be marked by service.

Then he beckons a little child into their midst. 'Whoever welcomes one such child in my name welcomes me, and whoever welcomes me welcomes not me but the one who sent me.'

This is an incredible saying. Jesus says that in welcoming a little child we are welcoming him. Elsewhere he says that if we want to enter the kingdom of God, then we must become like little children (Mark 10:15).

To live our lives as children means to let go of influence and power. It means to rediscover wonder and simplicity. It means to rediscover dependency. This also goes against the grain of the world. Aren't we supposed to be independent and grown-up?

While the world turns children into adults, Jesus is busy trying to turn adults back into children—children of a loving, heavenly father. Christian character means getting smaller, not bigger; choosing the last place, not the first.

Many people confuse character and personality. Personality is something we are born with. It may grow and change over the years, but all of us have different personalities that are simply part of who we are. Character is something else. Character is created by the choices we make about how we live our lives. Christian character means to choose to be Christ-like in everything we think and say and do. It is not easy. Its first step involves letting go of the desire to be great.

Generosity

'Whoever is not against us is for us. For truly I tell you, whoever gives you a cup of water to drink because you bear the name of Christ will by no means lose the reward' (Mark 9:40–41). These striking words of Jesus cut two ways. First, Jesus implies that if we follow him then we may be the ones who need to be given a cup of water. Bearing the name of Christ and trying to live Christ-like lives will mean hardship at times and will require from us sacrifice.

This is particularly hard in an affluent society like ours. The temptation is to allow the gospel to change some of our attitudes but to leave others unaffected. It has often been said that the last part of a human being to be converted is the wallet! But if we bear the name of Christ, then we must allow all of our life to be shaped by the values and standards of the gospel, and this will mean looking hard at the way we spend our money. Whether we like it or not, the way we spend our money speaks very eloquently of our priorities. To put it bluntly, if we spend more money each year on a daily newspaper, or on alcohol or evenings out or holidays, than on supporting the life of the church or supporting charities to alleviate suffering in the world, then very clearly those things take a higher priority in our lives than God.

This, then, is the second meaning of Jesus' words: we need to be the ones who are giving from the abundance of what we enjoy. In giving a cup of water to others, we give it to Christ, because Jesus is to be found in the poor and needy.

Generosity is not measured by how much we give, but by how much we have left after we have given. The poor widow in Mark 12:41–44 who, from her poverty, gave all that she had to live on contributed more than those who, from their abundance, gave a lot but also kept a lot back.

Children freely give whatever they have and share willingly

We also need to get involved in helping to build God's kingdom in the world, expressing our concern for the poor not just through giving money, but also in giving of our time and energy…

The Bible is very clear about all this… The prophets in the Old Testament rage against Israel, complaining again and again that the people worry about the finer points of religious observance while ignoring the plight of the oppressed and the poor.

In the New Testament, too, Jesus has a bias for the poor. The heroes of the Gospels are not usually the disciples but the little ones on the edge of the story. They are Jesus' chosen ones—the ones who understand who he is and are faithful to his call. Peter blunders in and gets it wrong, following his own will, his character unchanged by the gospel. The little ones who know their need of God are true citizens of the kingdom… But they are great not because they are small or innocent, but because their powerlessness gives them a freedom that adults usually lose. Children freely give whatever they have and share willingly, and they freely receive. We need to learn this same child-like attitude to life.

As our character is shaped by the gospel, there will times when we are thirsty and, in our vulnerability, will need others to minister to us. This requires of us boldness to follow where Christ calls, and humility to receive from others. Then there will be times when we are the ones who are called to give, and we must embrace this ministry with joy. It requires our money and our life.

To order a copy of this book, please turn to the order form on page 159.

The People's Bible Commentary

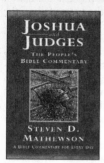

In the Hebrew Scriptures, Joshua and Judges join the books of Samuel and Kings as 'former prophets'. As prophetic books, they aim to challenge, indict and inspire God's people. The authors drew from events of the past to challenge a later generation of God's people about the way to live before God, and they call us today to clear up our picture of God and then to adjust our lives accordingly. This PBC volume is written by the Revd Dr Steven D. Mathewson, Senior Pastor of Dry Creek Bible Church in Belgrade, Montana, USA.

JUDGES 16:23–31

VICTORY *in* DEATH

The setting of the final scene in the Samson story has shifted from the prison to the temple. Philistine leaders have gathered to praise their god, Dagon, for victory over Samson (v. 23). Dagon was the god of grain and the chief deity of the Philistines. The term 'praised' in verse 24 is the Hebrew term *halal*, used throughout the psalms in reference to the praise of Yahweh. However, the 'psalm of praise' sung here is offered to Dagon. The Philistines' praise was based on victory at last over one who had ravaged their country and killed many of their people.

At the height of their celebration, the Philistines called for Samson to be brought out of the prison to entertain them. The verbs 'entertain' (v. 25) and 'performed' (vv. 25, 27) are both variations of a Hebrew verb which means 'to laugh'. They brought out Samson, then, to poke fun at him and to and to laugh at him as he stood blind between the two temple pillars.

Samson is a pathetic sight, yet he has a plan. In verse 26, he speaks to the attendant (literally, 'young man') who was assigned to help him. He asks the young man to help him feel the pillars between which he stood so that he could lean on them. These pillars, likely cedar columns on stone bases, would have been located in the centre of the temple to provide the main support for the roof. At this point, the narrator pauses the action to provide some important background information (v. 27). The temple was packed with about 3000 people, including all the leaders of the Philistines.

Samson's prayer and final cry

Positioned now between the pillars, Samson calls out to Yawheh (v. 28). He begins by addressing him as 'Lord GOD'—in Hebrew, *Adonai Yahweh*. The name Adonai means 'lord' or 'master' and stresses God's sovereignty. The name Yahweh is God's personal name by which his people knew him It stresses his ongoing care and his willingness to act in his people's behalf. After the address, Samson asks Yahweh to 'remember' him and 'strengthen' him. The term 'remember' does not imply forgetfulness on the part of Yahweh. Rather, it emphasizes taking notice of or taking action on behalf of someone. Interestingly, the purpose of Samson's request seems to be personal vengeance—repaying the Philistines for gouging out his eyes.

Regardless of Samson's motives, Yahweh responds! With attention to detail, the narrator carefully describes how Samson grasped the two middle pillars and leaned his weight on them with the use of his hands (v. 29). Then, Samson spoke his final words: 'Let me die with the Philistines.' What a tragic reversal of events! The man set apart to Yahweh for the deliverance of Israel can only hope to die with the enemy. Verse 30 relates the action concisely. Samson pushed with all his might, and the house fell on the entire cast of Philistines. Here, the narrator adds a brilliant observation: Samson killed more Philistines in his death than he did in his entire life (v. 30). The details in verse 31 indicate that his relatives honoured him in death by bringing his body home and burying it in the family tomb. The Samson story then closes with the note that 'he had judged Israel twenty years'.

Faithful God, unfaithful people

The Samson story provides a sobering reminder that Yahweh will accomplish his purposes whether or not his people cooperate. Samson accomplishes more as a deliverer in his death then he did in his life. The truth is, unfaithfulness on the part of God's people does not hinder God, but it proves to be tragic for God's people. Samson resembles the nation of Israel by leaving his special calling and using his privileges to satisfy his own desires. When God's people fail to seek first his kingdom, they end up paying a tragic price. This story, then, confirms the message of the book: God's people disintegrate when they abandon God's standards to follow the values of the pagan culture around them.

Prayer

Father, all that I have, all that I am, all that I hope to be, I give to you. Help me to use all you have given me to further your kingdom.

Jacob's dream

Lucy Moore

The sun had set over the desert
and stars pricked the sky overhead.
'I can't see my way in the darkness—
I'll spend the night here,' Jacob said.
He wanted to hide in a cave,
as his conscience was wild as the sea.
'The crimes of the past will not
   let my mind rest
And I know how hard sleeping
   will be.

But I'm blowed if I'll skulk in a
corner! I might well have run
   from my home,
But I'll face up to God like the
man that I am. He can love me
   or leave me alone.'
So he pulled out a rock for a pillow
and lay in the cool open air.
'I am rotten right through,
   but I'm honest with you.
Here I am, God, if you're there.'

God didn't mess with young Jacob.
He switched him out just like a light
And clicked with his fingers for music,
and rubbed both his hands and said,
   'Right!'
He drew back the curtain that shields
us from the dazzling blaze of his home,

Gave Jacob a shake so he felt
   wide awake
And stood back to watch from
   his throne.

And Jacob's dream-eyes snapped
wide open at the huge movie screen
   of the sky,
For there up above him were angels,
some thirty or forty foot high,
Like rainbows in rainbows in
rainbows, with wings like the top
   fighter jets
And muscles like melons and hair
   with gold gel on,
Their faces like soldiers', calm, set.

Not one of these mystical giants
stood still; they all moved with
   purpose and power
From heaven to earth on a staircase
or ramp reaching up through the
   skies like a tower.
And then earth to heaven returning
they traced their steps up once again,
An army patrolling, earth's nations
   controlling,
This would boggle your mind
   but ah! then—

Jacob saw at the top of the staircase
none other than God the almighty!
He trembled and tossed in his sleep
where he lay, clutching the hem
    of his nightie.
He hadn't imagined that God was
so BIG! Hadn't thought him so
    powerful either,
But the voice of the Lord soon
    reassured him:
'I am the God of your father.

I will give you the land where you're
lying; your children will spread out
    like dust.
All people on earth will find blessings
through you from the north, south
    and east and the west.
I am with you right now and
wherever you go, be sure I will watch
    over you.
I will bring you back here, Jacob,
    no need to fear,
I won't leave you till all this
    comes true.'

And Jacob woke up hot and sweaty,
although the night air was so chill.
'I didn't know God was that near me!
Crumbs! He must be near me still!
This must be the gateway to heaven,
though the staircase is hid
    from me now.
I can't sleep a wink; I need all night
    to think.
In the morning, I'll make God a vow.'

So he picked up his rock and he
stood it on end just as the sun started
    to shine,
No longer a pillow for dreamers,
but a pillar to stand as a sign.

'If you watch over me, keep me fed
and well-clothed and bring me safe
    home to my dad,
You can be my God too, and I'll pay
    up to you
A tenth of my earnings—not bad!'

When Jacob made bargains like that
with his God, how funny God must've
    been feeling!
But I'm sure God loved taking him
just as he was, with all of his
    wheeling and dealing.
Though Isaac and Abraham knew
God, without dreaming dreams
    on a stone,
Because God's great plan would be
    worked through this man,
Jake had to know God for his own.

I wonder, if my eyes were opened,
if the eyes of my soul weren't so dim,
Would I see a staircase before me,
going up from my town straight
    to Him?
If I saw all those angels down my
street, striding from heaven to me,
Then how would I feel? Would it
    make God more real?
How much on this earth we can't see!

Lucy Moore is BRF's Barnabas
Ministry Representative for the
South of England. She is the author
of *The Gospels Unplugged*, a book of
52 poems and stories for creative
writing, RE, drama and collective
worship.

New Daylight © BRF 2003

The Bible Reading Fellowship
First Floor, Elsfield Hall, 15–17 Elsfield Way, Oxford OX2 8FG
ISBN 1 84101 042 1

Distributed in Australia by:
Willow Connection, PO Box 288, Brookvale, NSW 2100.
Tel: 02 9948 3957; Fax: 02 9948 8153;
E-mail: info@willowconnection.com.au
Available also from all good Christian bookshops in Australia.
For individual and group subscriptions in Australia:
Mrs Rosemary Morrall, PO Box W35, Wanniassa, ACT 2903.

Distributed in New Zealand by:
Scripture Union Wholesale, PO Box 760, Wellington
Tel: 04 385 0421; Fax: 04 384 3990; E-mail: suwholesale@clear.net.nz

Distributed in South Africa by:
Struik Book Distributors, PO Box 193, Maitland 7405, Cape Town
Tel: 021 551 5900; Fax: 021 551 1124; E-mail: enquiries@struik.co.za

Distributed in the USA by:
The Bible Reading Fellowship, PO Box 380, Winter Park,
Florida 32790-0380
Tel: 407 628 4330 or 800 749 4331; Fax: 407 647 2406;
E-mail: brf@biblereading.org; Website: www.biblereading.org

Publications distributed to more than 60 countries

Acknowledgments

Printed in Denmark

SUPPORTING BRF'S MINISTRY

BRF seeks to help people of all ages to experience the living God—Father, Son and Holy Spirit—at a deeper level, and enable them to grow as disciples of Jesus Christ through the Bible, prayer and worship.

We need your help if we are to make a real impact on the local church and community. In an increasingly secular world people need even more help with their Bible reading, their prayer and their discipleship. We can do something about this, but our resources are limited. With your help, if we all do a little, together we can make a huge difference.

How can you help?

• You could become a *Friend of BRF* and encourage BRF's ministry within your own church and community (contact the BRF office, or visit the BRF website, www.brf.org.uk).

• You could support BRF's ministry with a donation or standing order (using the response form overleaf).

• You could consider making a bequest to BRF in your will, and so give lasting support to our work. (We have a leaflet available with more information about this, which can be requested using the form overleaf.)

• And, most important of all, you could become a BRF *Prayer Partner* and support BRF with your prayers. *Prayer Partners* receive our bi-monthly prayer letter which includes details of all that is going on within BRF and specific prayer pointers for each prayer need. (To become a *Prayer Partner* write to BRF or e-mail enquiries@brf.org.uk)

Whatever you can do or give, we thank you for your support.

BRF MINISTRY APPEAL RESPONSE FORM

Name _____

Address _____

_____ Postcode _____

Telephone _____ Email _____

(tick as appropriate)

Gift Aid Declaration

☐ I am a UK taxpayer. I want BRF to treat as Gift Aid Donations all donations I make from the date of this declaration until I notify you otherwise.

Signature _____ Date _____

☐ I would like to support BRF's ministry with a regular donation by standing order (please complete the Banker's Order below).

Standing Order – Banker's Order

To the Manager, Name of Bank/Building Society _____

Address _____

_____ Postcode _____

Sort Code _____ Account Name _____

Account No _____

Please pay Royal Bank of Scotland plc, London Drummonds Branch, 49 Charing Cross, London SW1A 2DX (Sort Code 16-00-38), for the account of BRF A/C No. 00774151

The sum of _____ pounds on ___ /___ /___ (insert date your standing order starts) and thereafter the same amount on the same day of each month until further notice.

Signature _____ Date _____

Single donation

☐ I enclose my cheque/credit card/Switch card details for a donation of £5 £10 £25 £50 £100 £250 (other) £ _____ to support BRF's ministry

Credit/ Switch card no. ☐☐☐☐☐☐☐☐☐☐☐☐☐☐☐☐☐☐☐

Expires ☐☐ ☐☐   Issue no. of Switch card ☐☐☐

Signature _____ Date _____

(Where appropriate, on receipt of your donation, we will send you a Gift Aid form)

☐ Please send me information about making a bequest to BRF in my will.

Please detach and send this completed form to: Richard Fisher, BRF, First Floor, Elsfield Hall, 15–17 Elsfield Way, Oxford OX2 8FG. BRF is a Registered Charity (No.233280)

A pack of resources and ideas to help to promote Bible reading in your church is available from BRF. The pack, which will be of use at any time during the year, includes sample editions of the notes, magazine articles, leaflets about BRF Bible reading resources and much more. Unless you specify the month in which you would like the pack sent, we will send it immediately on receipt of your order. We greatly appreciate your donations towards the cost of producing the pack (without them we would not be able to make the pack available) and we welcome your comments about the contents of the pack and your ideas for future ones.

This coupon should be sent to:

BRF
First Floor
Elsfield Hall
15–17 Elsfield Way
Oxford
OX2 8FG

Name ————————————————————————

Address ——————————————————————————

————————————————————————————————

———————————————————————— Postcode —————————

Telephone ——————————————————————

Email ——————————————————————————————

Please send me ———— Bible Reading Resources Pack(s)

Please send the pack now/ in ———————————— (month).

I enclose a donation for £ ———— towards the cost of the pack.

NDMay03   BRF is a Registered Charity

NEW DAYLIGHT SUBSCRIPTIONS

☐ I would like to give a gift subscription (please complete both name and address sections below)

☐ I would like to take out a subscription myself (complete name and address details only once)

This completed coupon should be sent with appropriate payment to BRF. Alternatively, please write to us quoting your name, address, the subscription you would like for either yourself or a friend (with their name and address), the start date and credit card number, expiry date and signature if paying by credit card.

Gift subscription name _____

Gift subscription address_____

_____

_____Postcode _____

Please send beginning with the September 2003/January/May 2004 issue: (delete as applicable)

(please tick box)

	UK	SURFACE	AIR MAIL
NEW DAYLIGHT	☐ £11.10	☐ £12.45	☐ £14.70
NEW DAYLIGHT 3-year sub	☐ £27.45		
NEW DAYLIGHT LARGE PRINT	☐ £16.80	☐ £20.40	☐ £24.90

Please complete the payment details below and send your coupon, with appropriate payment to: **BRF, First Floor, Elsfield Hall, 15–17 Elsfield Way, Oxford OX2 8FG.**

Your name_____

Your address_____

_____

_____Postcode _____

Total enclosed £ _____ (cheques should be made payable to 'BRF')

Payment by cheque ☐ postal order ☐ Visa ☐ Mastercard ☐ Switch ☐

Card number: ☐☐☐☐☐☐☐☐☐☐☐☐☐☐☐☐☐☐☐

Expiry date of card: ☐☐☐☐   Issue number (Switch): ☐☐☐☐

Signature (essential if paying by credit/Switch card)_____

☐ Please do not send me further information about BRF publications.

NDMay03   BRF is a Registered Charity

BRF PUBLICATIONS ORDER FORM

Please ensure that you complete and send off both sides of this order form.

Please send me the following book(s):		Quantity	Price	Total
235 1	(Extra)Ordinary Women (C. Blake)	_____	£6.99	_____
238 6	On This Rock (S. Cottrell)	_____	£3.99	_____
Barnabas				
243 2	The Gospels Unplugged (L. Moore)	_____	£12.99	_____
332 3	Bible Make and Do 1 (G. Chapman)	_____	£5.99	_____
333 1	Bible Make and Do 2 (G. Chapman)	_____	£5.99	_____
People's Bible Commentary				
095 2	PBC: Joshua and Judges (S. Mathewson)	_____	£7.99	_____
030 8	PBC: 1 & 2 Samuel (H. Mowvley)	_____	£7.99	_____
118 5	PBC: 1 & 2 Kings (S. Dawes)	_____	£7.99	_____
070 7	PBC: Chronicles—Nehemiah (M. Tunnicliffe)	_____	£7.99	_____
094 4	PBC: Job (K. Dell)	_____	£7.99	_____
031 6	PBC: Psalms 1—72 (D. Coggan)	_____	£7.99	_____
065 0	PBC: Psalms 73—150 (D. Coggan)	_____	£7.99	_____
071 5	PBC: Proverbs (E. Mellor)	_____	£7.99	_____
087 1	PBC: Jeremiah (R. Mason)	_____	£7.99	_____
040 5	PBC: Ezekiel (E. Lucas)	_____	£7.99	_____
028 6	PBC: Nahum—Malachi (G. Emmerson)	_____	£7.99	_____
191 6	PBC: Matthew (J. Proctor)	_____	£7.99	_____
046 4	PBC: Mark (D. France)	_____	£7.99	_____
027 8	PBC: Luke (H. Wansbrough)	_____	£7.99	_____
029 4	PBC: John (R.A. Burridge)	_____	£7.99	_____
082 0	PBC: Romans (J. Dunn)	_____	£7.99	_____
122 3	PBC: 1 Corinthians (J. Murphy-O'Connor)	_____	£7.99	_____
073 1	PBC: 2 Corinthians (A. Besançon Spencer)	_____	£7.99	_____
012 X	PBC: Galatians and 1 & 2 Thessalonians (J. Fenton)	_____	£7.99	_____
047 2	PBC: Ephesians—Colossians & Philemon (M. Maxwell)	_____	£7.99	_____
119 3	PBC: Timothy, Titus and Hebrews (D. France)	_____	£7.99	_____
092 8	PBC: James—Jude (F. Moloney)	_____	£7.99	_____
3297 5	PBC: Revelation (M. Maxwell)	_____	£7.99	_____

Total cost of books £ _____

Postage and packing (see over) £ _____

TOTAL £ _____

See over for payment details. All prices are correct at time of going to press, are subject to the prevailing rate of VAT and may be subject to change without prior warning.

NDMay03   The Bible Reading Fellowship is a Registered Charity

PAYMENT DETAILS

Please complete the payment details below and send with appropriate payment and completed order form to:

BRF, First Floor, Elsfield Hall,
15–17 Elsfield Way, Oxford OX2 8FG

Name _____

Address _____

_____

_____ Postcode _____

Telephone _____

Email _____

Total enclosed £ _____ (cheques should be made payable to 'BRF')

Payment by cheque ☐ postal order ☐ Visa ☐ Mastercard ☐ Switch ☐

Card number: ☐☐☐☐☐☐☐☐☐☐☐☐☐☐☐☐☐☐

Expiry date of card: ☐☐☐☐   Issue number (Switch): ☐☐☐☐

Signature (essential if paying by credit/Switch card) _____

ALTERNATIVE WAYS TO ORDER

Christian bookshops: All good Christian bookshops stock BRF publications. For your nearest stockist, please contact BRF.

POSTAGE AND PACKING CHARGES				
order value	UK	Europe	Surface	Air Mail
£7.00 & under	£1.25	£3.00	£3.50	£5.50
£7.01–£30.00	£2.25	£5.50	£6.50	£10.00
Over £30.00	free	prices on request		

Telephone: The BRF office is open between 09.15 and 17.00.
To place your order, phone 01865 319700; fax 01865 319701.

Web: Visit www.brf.org.uk

☐ Please do not send me further information about BRF publications.

BRF is a Registered Charity